The Warm Kitchen

Gluten-Free Recipes Anyone Can Make and Everyone Will Love

Robert + Family —
I hope you enjoy the
book! Hopefully it inspires
you.
Amy Fothergill

Over 150 Recipes with Dairy and Egg Substitutions

Amy Fothergill

Copyright ©2013 by Amy Fothergill

Photography by Amy, Alan, and Santo Fothergill ©2013, Carina Woudenberg ©2011 and Regan Daniels (headshots) ©2013

Editors: Jennifer Gonsalves, Carol Hunter, Gabrielle Su, Jill Ohline, Karen Paskow, Jackie Ferris, and Lisa West.

Design: Cuniberti Design; Redwood City, California

Cover design: Rafael DeSoto, Jr.

Production: Daniel Drenger; New York, NY

ISBN 978-0-9894843-0-5

Published in the United States by The Family Chef Publishing,
PO Box 953, Half Moon Bay, CA, 94019, USA.
For questions or to contact the author, you can send an e-mail to amy@amythefamilychef.com or send a letter to the address above.

Printed in the United States by Bang Printing.

This book is dedicated to my mother who knew I had talent in the kitchen from a young age. Thanks Mom; I know you would be proud and wish you were here to see me.

Acknowledgments

I'm not sure where to start with this one; there are so many people to thank. Being "the family chef", I have to start with my immediate family first. Thank you to my husband Alan, for being supportive with this project in so many ways. Thank you to my kids, Santo and Kate, for enduring recipe testing, food photography ("don't eat that yet! I need a picture."), shopping trips to the grocery store, and more. Thanks especially to my son who actually took some of the photos. He has a good eye!

The next set of thank yous goes to the rest of my family. No matter what house we cook in, there is always a feeling of warmth and love in our kitchens. I often felt like they thought I was crazy when I started cooking gluten-free but in the end, they have been very supportive. My mother, who always had something cooking on the stove, was the one who saw something in me at a young age and encouraged me to attend the Cornell School of Hotel Administration, something truly memorable and life-changing. So much of my cooking is a reflection of her. My dad left us way too young but instilled a sense of confidence in me which I didn't find until later in life. Now, when I stand in front of a crowd and tell stories, I think of him. My siblings, Lisa and Anthony, have been amazing, even though they used to tell me I came from the circus when I was very young. Aunt Lorraine is like a second mother to me, and Uncle Frank a second father. My cousin Lenny (no, not Vinny) has always been there to support me, make me laugh, and enjoy my food. To my other cousin, Gina, thank you for being my cheerleader and make-up artist when we were younger. I know they are all proud of me.

To my friends, especially Christine who donned me The Family Chef, although I don't see you very often, you are always in my thoughts. To Jenn, your help with this project and friendship has been greatly appreciated. To Lisa, who has been the recipient of many a test recipe, is most importantly a good listener and great friend. To Michele, who has encouraged me from the start and joined the gluten-free wagon, I appreciate you reminding me to celebrate the little successes. To Sheri, who I admire so much, thank you for being a good friend and also a cheerleader. To Alison, whose culinary wonders inspire me, thank you for your support and your friendship. To Nancy, who got me started on this project and will hopefully be able to support me by selling a few books. To Dayna, for being such a supportive friend and for her great feedback. To Mary Claire, thank you for believing in me and always being supportive. To Melanie, your soulful perspective has truly inspired me. To Amy A., who brought me gluten-free inspiration early on in the process.

To Jeanne, thank you for your encouragement, support, and friendship over the past few years; even though most of it was virtual until recently. The Foreword that you wrote about me and this book means so much and has given me a renewed energy. Your recipes and words are amazing!

Almost all of these pictures (except two) have been taken by myself, my husband, or my son (then 7 years old). Most of them were taken in my kitchen. I hope your food looks just as good.

To Carol, whose editing skills and use of the comma, still amaze me. To my other editors, Gabbie, Lisa, Jill, and Karen, thank you so much for your time! Thank you to Carina, for helping me with my projects along with some of the editing as well, including being quite eloquent with the wording on the back cover.

A big thanks to all of my recipe testers: Karen and Cherie (my top two testers and positive reinforcers), Gabbie (pulling a close third with enthusiasm), Jackie, Denise, Jill, Gretchen, Jenny, Lisa, Tanya, Sarah, Joe, Melanie, Pam, Kristen, Rebecca, Melinda, Shamalah-Allah, Hannah, Robyn, Carla, and Michele. If there were others, thank you as well (that's quite a list!).

To the Cornell Hotel School, for accepting my application and changing my culinary life. I still have fond memories of lighting a gas stove (something I still don't like to do), identifying pieces of meat on a table in a walk-in, learning about wine, our "cookies" class, and more. It was an unforgettable experience that helped pave the way for The Family Chef.

To Lea and Dan, the wonderful designer and production artist/retoucher who did the layout, for taking my vision of a book and transforming it into something beautiful, which you see on these pages. It is stunning because of both of you.

To Celia, for taking the time to help me find "the warm kitchen." I'm very happy to have reconnected with you.

To anyone whom I have forgotten and everyone who has influenced me, listened, advised, tested, helped, and generally supported me, Thank You!

"Good food with family and friends is what makes a warm kitchen."

–Amy Fothergill

Table of Contents

Foreword

The Warm Kitchen by Amy Fothergill is a wonderful addition to the gluten-free kitchen's bookshelf. To be honest, it would be a lovely part of anyone's kitchen—gluten-free or not. As you begin to use it, it will probably take pride of place in yours as it does in mine. And this is not just a cookbook—it is so much more. It is also an easy-to-use reference guide and how-to manual that is terrific for gluten-free newbies as well as those of us who are farther along in our gluten-free journey and know the ropes.

One thing I love about this book—and that distinguishes it from others of its kind—is that Amy knows the importance of technique. She is a trained chef and has learned how to use her ingredients to their best advantage. I have found over and over again in gluten-free cooking and baking that the best ingredients can sometimes create sub-par results when you don't know the optimal ways to prepare them. This doesn't mean that Amy's recipes are fussy or difficult—far from it—but it does mean that she knows what she's doing. In addition, she knows how to communicate these techniques clearly and concisely as she walks her readers through the important steps that turn a 'hum-drum' recipe into a "I want to make this every week" recipe.

In addition to being a trained and working chef, Amy is a mom with a busy family. Known as The Family Chef, she applies her culinary training to the task of creating delicious and easy-to-prepare meals for the whole family. The recipes in this book create yummy, satisfying, and healthful meals and treats that are appealing to everyone. This makes this book perfect for anyone who wants good tasting recipes that work (she had a range of testers for all of her recipes) and that appeal to a range of eaters (adults to kids).

On top of everything else, Amy also provides tips and guidelines along the way for how to: save time; change the flavor profile of a basic dish; use several different sizes of pans; choose ingredients; stock your pantry; detect hidden gluten; and adapt your recipes further to accommodate dairy-free, nut-free, egg-free, and sugar-free eaters. I am an experienced gluten-free cook and baker and I found myself saying over and over again, "wow, what a good idea" to her delectable morsels of advice.

The Warm Kitchen is a celebration of gluten-free cooking, baking, and eating. It welcomes everyone into the kitchen and tempts folks from the most timid of cooks to kitchen pros to come in, put on an apron, and start cooking delicious food. Enjoy!

Jeanne Sauvage
Gluten-Free Baking for the Holidays: 60 Recipes for Traditional Festive Treats
Art of Gluten-Free Baking blog

April 24, 2013

Foreword | THE WARM KITCHEN   **9**

Notes on Pantry Sections

BULK BIN FOODS, GRAINS, AND CANNED FOODS

If you are gluten intolerant or have celiac disease, it is not advisable to buy from the bulk bin of a grocery store. The item you are buying can be contaminated with gluten from another bin such as flour, barley or wheat berries, regardless of where it's positioned. Buying a sealed bag is safer. You should still check with the manufacturer about their processing practices to make sure traces of gluten have not gotten into the food.

Gluten can even be in canned beans and some normally gluten-free grains like buckwheat if the manufacturer is not careful. These are often hidden places for gluten.

If you are only gluten sensitive, you may not have to be as diligent. This is a personal decision.

OTHER DRY GOODS

Another potentially hidden place for gluten is in soy milk and broth, specifically chicken broth. Look at the ingredients and look for barley, hydrolyzed wheat gluten or wheat protein.

Make sure any product you buy does not contain malt like malt vinegar or malt flavoring; this is a derivative of barley so it has gluten in it. Malt flavoring and wheat starch can both be found in some of your favorite breakfast cereals.

Read all of the ingredients of your ketchups, mustards, etc. Make sure you buy gluten-free soy sauce as well as hoisin, oyster, and curry sauces.

Spices can also be contaminated with gluten. Look for a gluten-free certification or learn which brands are gluten-free.

OATS: GLUTEN-FREE OR NOT?

Oats often confuse people. Are they gluten-free or not? Oats do not inherently have gluten; however, two things can cause them to not be gluten-free: they can be grown next to gluten grains like wheat, barley or rye, and they can be processed on the same machines as these grains. Gluten-free oats are available but there are some people, usually those who have celiac disease, who cannot tolerate any oats. There is something about the protein that their body cannot process. Most recipes in the book have substitutions.

GLUTEN-FREE PASTAS

It is true; not all gluten-free pastas are created equal. Try different brands and shapes. There are different types of pasta such as corn, quinoa, and brown rice, as well as blends of potato, soy, and rice. Make sure to read the section

Gluten-Free Pasta Cooking Tips (see Index). If you haven't had a lot of success with gluten-free dried pasta, these tips will help. My favorite brands are Bionaturae® and Tinkyada®. I keep my pasta drawer well stocked with pastas like elbow, penne, spaghetti, lasagna, and rotini. You can even find ditalini (great for soups) and rice gnocchi.

WHAT NOT TO KEEP

- Regular soy sauce, teriyaki sauce, and any sauce or salad dressing with regular soy sauce
- Anything with malt vinegar, malt flavoring, or malt seasoning
- Wheat germ and wheat bran
- Non-certified oats (depending upon your level of sensitivity)
- Anything with spelt, kamut, semolina, or triticale
- Candy or ice cream with cookies, wafers or any form of gluten
- Anything with modified food starch if it's made from wheat
- Beer, unless it is gluten-free

Gluten-Free Flours and Starches

Gluten-free flours are ground-up grains like brown rice, millet, and quinoa. There are also starches like cornstarch, potato and tapioca starch, which are used to help thicken sauces and add balance to flour blends. Today, it's easy to find these flours and starches in most natural foods stores or on-line. I do not refrigerate mine, but I live in an area with moderate temperatures. Use your judgment or follow the recommendation on the label.

When I first went gluten-free, I had all of these flours in my cabinet because so many recipes called for 2-8 of them (yes, 8; that was a little crazy). One of the goals of this cookbook is to streamline the number of flours you keep on hand as well as to teach you how to use them. One reason that I make my own desserts is that many of the gluten-free mixes do not contain enough whole grains (in my opinion); they primarily contain white rice flour, potato starch and/or tapioca starch. It is fine to use these ingredients but too much of it can cause your blood sugar to rise; I'm not a dietitian but I believe most will tell you that is true!

Here are some of the ones I keep in my kitchen and why, along with a few others.

MY FAVORITES:

- Brown rice flour-This is a staple in my flour blend.
- White rice flour-I use this flour in some recipes and for "flouring" chicken.
- Millet flour-This is another integral part of my flour blend. It gives baked goods a slightly yellow color. If you don't like that, use less in the blend mix or add in some white rice flour.
- Sorghum flour-This is the perfect flour for bread, pizza and some other baked goods.
- Buckwheat flour-I use this flour in crepes, pancakes and bread. Make sure it's certified gluten-free if you are intolerant to gluten.
- Teff flour-I use this flour mostly for bread to give my "white" bread more of a whole grain look. I also use it occasionally in pancakes and/or waffles.
- Almond flour-This "flour" is really just finely ground blanched almonds so if you have a powerful food processor or blender, you can make your own. It works well in cookies. Store this in the fridge.
- Tapioca flour (or starch)-I have read that the starch and flour are the same and I have read they are different; I consider them the same. I use it in my flour blend and for certain recipes.
- Potato starch (not flour)-Make sure you don't confuse potato flour with potato starch. The flour smells like instant potatoes and the starch is more mild. I use the starch in my flour blend and for certain recipes.
- Cornstarch-A readily accessible ingredient that is one of the best thickeners for sauces, gravies and soups.

OTHER/OCCASIONAL FLOURS

- Amaranth flour-This is a whole grain flour with a nutty taste.
- Quinoa flour-This flour is nutrient rich but does not always work well as a flour substitute. Use it in conjunction with a rice-based flour and at least one starch.
- Garbanzo bean flour or Garfava flour-This flour works well in dishes like cornbread and falafel but can give the batter a funny taste. Don't taste the batter; the end result is usually fine.
- Potato flour-It can be a good thickener for soups.
- Corn flour-This flour is the finely milled version of the whole corn kernel. It can be used in baking.
- Chestnut flour-Not readily available in the United States, but you might see it in specialty stores. This nutty-flavored flour works well in baked goods.
- Coconut flour-This flour has a high protein content but it absorbs more liquid which might affect your baked goods. Experiment with it.
- Arrowroot-A very good substitute for cornstarch in baked goods or as a thickener.

Common Substitutions

When you switch to a gluten-free diet, you may think you will never have that comfy "warm kitchen" feeling again. That's not the case. I explain it to people like language and being immersed. If someone dropped you off in a foreign country and you did not know how to speak, it would be rough in the beginning but you would eventually learn. Instead of saying "hello", you might say "hola", "ciao" or "guten tag". Instead of flour, there are alternatives like brown rice flour, millet flour, cornstarch, and potato starch. You can do this!

A few years ago, this immersion could have been a lonely journey; that is certainly how I felt when there were not as many resources and products. Today, it's not too bad. It is no longer necessary to learn from scratch. Plus, I'm hoping this cookbook will be your new translation resource.

After working in business, one thing that I have learned is if you use repeatable processes, you can be more efficient. The same is true in cooking and baking. Using a pre-mixed gluten-free flour blend takes the burden out of gluten-free baking. Grabbing white rice flour instead of regular flour when breading chicken will become second nature. It all gets easier.

In this section, I have included most of the common substitutions for ingredients that have gluten as well as other common allergens; dairy and eggs. Nuts are almost always optional and I don't use a lot of soy. By learning this new "language" of gluten-free, your kitchen can be a warm kitchen again.

HOW TO MAKE

Amy's Gluten-Free Flour Blend

This is the flour blend that will hopefully change your life. It's easy to mix, versatile, and can be a substitute for flour in almost any recipe.

MIX TOGETHER AND KEEP IN AN AIR TIGHT CONTAINER:

- 3 cups brown rice flour
- 1 cup tapioca flour or starch
- 1 cup potato starch (not flour)
- 1 cup millet flour

Note: If you can't find or don't want to use millet flour, substitute with an equal amount of white rice or brown rice flour.

One thing that I noticed was some recipes and products (just look at the label) use a lot of "white" flour, for example white rice, potato, and tapioca starch. It might produce a decent product but falls short on the nutrition scale. I like this blend that I created because it provides whole grain from the brown rice and millet flours; thank you to my friend, Amy Andrews of Amy's Food Room, for the inspiration. The upside is that it is light enough to create a baked good with excellent texture. Also, when I'm measuring if I have a little more or a little less, I don't fret. When I measure the flour for a recipe, I'm more precise.

I use this blend as an all-purpose flour for almost everything with a few exceptions. I found it is much easier to measure out my flours once a month or so and then just scoop out what I need when I'm cooking or baking. It makes the whole immersion into gluten-free a much smoother transition. If you do not need to use gluten-free flour, most of the recipes can be substituted with all-purpose flour; just omit the xanthan gum.

The good news is that once you make this blend, you may not need any other gluten-free flours. That is my goal. I want it to be easy for you. Personally, I still need a few others for my baking and cooking but for the most part, this is what I use. I use Bob's Red Mill® flours, starches, and xanthan gum. It's easy to find and has worked well for these recipes. I prefer my blend to most other blends on the market.

The rule of thumb when converting your own recipes is to substitute this blend 1:1 with the flour in a recipe. However, to help hold it together for baking and add a nice crumb, add ½ teaspoon of xanthan gum or ¾ teaspoon of guar gum for every 2 cups of the flour when making quick breads and

cakes. For pizzas, breads, and cookies, use 1 teaspoon of xanthan gum or 1½ teaspoons of guar gum for every 2 cups of the flour blend. Try this conversion with your own recipes.

The last bit of advice in regards to baking is to always mix the batter briskly for about 10-15 seconds. With a regular batter, you don't want to develop the gluten. With gluten-free, you want the gum and starch to "gel". Mixing it with a few quick rotations will do the trick.

BINDERS

If you need to learn about thickeners for soups and sauces, read the *Making Sauces and Gravies* section (see Index). Slurries are used in place of a traditional butter and flour roux. A slurry also helps to decrease the amount of fat in a dish.

Many dishes like meatloaf and meatballs call for breadcrumbs to help bind the dish together. Today, you can find gluten-free breadcrumbs in many stores. Make sure to test it first; some brands are better than others. Another option is toasted, chopped gluten-free bread. You can also use crushed up gluten-free rice or corn flake cereal as well as gluten-free quick oats (as long as you can tolerate oats). Many of the recipes in the *Main Dishes* chapter outline how to do this (see Index).

BREADING AND BATTERS

When I first started cooking gluten-free, I avoided "flouring" my food because the flour mix became too thick and starchy. After a great tip from Jacqueline Mallorca, a true gluten-free expert, I learned that you can use white rice flour.

Another option, which I prefer, is to use equal parts of white rice flour and potato starch as a substitute to flour or dredge chicken or meat; it produces very good results. For example, if a recipe calls for 2 tablespoons of flour, use 1 tablespoon each of white rice flour and potato starch. Remember to always season it with salt and pepper.

The starch helps with thickening as well, so if broth or lemon juice is added to the pan, it will create its own sauce.

Many batters can be made with egg whites and cornstarch. See the recipes for *Fish and Chips* and *Coconut Shrimp* for how to make it (see Index).

As mentioned above in the BINDERS section, there are many substitutions these days for breadcrumbs. See the section *Other Ways to Cook Chicken Breast* for tips on how to make these substitutions (see Index). To substitute the eggs, use a combination of ground flaxseed and water (see the following page).

MAKING "BUTTERMILK"
(WITH REGULAR MILK OR MILK SUBSTITUTE)

I use buttermilk in many of my baked goods. Besides having a tangy flavor, the acid in the buttermilk helps with rising.

To make a replacement for 1 cup of buttermilk, place 1 tablespoon of white vinegar or lemon juice in a glass measuring cup. Add any type of milk (for example, regular, soy, or coconut) to measure 1 cup. Allow to sit for 5 minutes. This can be proportioned to make ½ cup or even ¾ cup.

Dairy, Egg, and Sugar Substitutes

Quite often, people who cannot eat gluten also have to omit other foods from their diet. The section below provides details for dairy (really casein, the protein found in milk), egg, and sugar substitutes.

DAIRY SUBSTITUTIONS: MILK AND SOUR CREAM

There are many alternative milks on the market these days. Some of the ones I use are almond, coconut, or rice (soy doesn't sit so well with me). Be careful because some soy milks can contain gluten (from a barley extract) so check the label.

For baking, if you use a sweetened alternative milk, you might need to reduce the sugar in the recipe by 2-3 tablespoons. My recipes generally are not very sugary so it might be ok to substitute without reducing the sugar. If you find the finished product sweet in anyway, it's acceptable to reduce the sugar. See previous page for a buttermilk substitute.

For cooking, use plain, unsweetened milk substitutes. Check the label to make sure there is no added sugar.

To make a sour cream substitute for cooking and baking, place 2 liquid tablespoons of shortening or plain coconut oil in a 1 cup glass measure. Heat if necessary to liquefy. Add 2 teaspoons white vinegar or lemon juice. Add enough milk substitute to measure 1 cup. Set aside for 5 minutes.

DAIRY SUBSTITUTIONS: BUTTER

For cooking, use olive or another vegetable oil instead. For something with more mouthfeel, use coconut oil.

For baking, use vegetable shortening (I like Spectrum's® organic vegetable shortening best) or coconut oil; I prefer the shortening. If you use the coconut oil, melt it first so it's easier to measure and mix. The virgin coconut has a coconut flavor. If you don't like that flavor, use the non-virgin.

Use vegetable shortening just like butter. If the recipe calls for melted butter, heat the shortening. If it calls for softened butter, heat slightly so it's easier

to work with. You do not need to refrigerate it. Some people also use Earth's Balance® sticks in place of butter; I do not use it very often. If you like this and can tolerate soy, this is a common substitution for butter.

For baking, you can usually substitute a vegetable oil like canola or sunflower for the butter, even if the recipe does not call for melted butter. I have successfully used canola oil instead of butter for cookies. The texture will be slightly different. Always test your recipe.

EGG SUBSTITUTIONS

When it comes to eggs, there are many substitutions including a egg replacer products by Ener-g brand® and Bob's Red Mill®. If you want to substitute eggs in quiche, look for a recipe with tofu.

Eggs provide different functions so the substitute can vary. Try some of these:

Leavening

1 egg = 2 teaspoons baking powder + 1 tablespoon warm water + 1 tablespoon oil (to double, use only 3 teaspoons of baking powder but double everything else)

This is my personal favorite for baking:
2 eggs = 5 tablespoons warm water + 1 tablespoon oil + 1 tablespoon ground flaxseed + 2 teaspoons baking powder (mix in a small bowl and wait 5-10 minutes).

Binding and Moisture

1 egg = 1 tablespoon ground flax seed + 2 tablespoons warm water + 1 tablespoon oil (mix well and let stand 10 minutes)
1 egg = ¼ cup applesauce or pureed fruit or ½ mashed banana
1 egg = 3 tablespoons nut butter

EGG SUBSTITUTIONS: MAYONNAISE

There are a number of mayonnaise substitutes if you can tolerate soy. Look for ones that are marked as vegan which means there is no dairy or eggs. Note: there is usually no dairy in mayonnaise; only eggs. Dairy refers to foods derived from cows.

SUGAR SUBSTITUTIONS

I try to use organic sugar or sugar cane whenever possible. For things like pancakes and waffles, you can easily substitute agave nectar, honey, maple syrup or brown rice syrup.

I do not use stevia, aspartame, or any artificial sweetener as I don't like the flavor. If you use these, you will need to test the recipe.

If you use a liquid sweetener like agave or honey, it will make baked products like cakes or muffins very wet. Try this substitution:
1 cup sugar = ¼ cup agave nectar or syrup + ½ cup sugar (white or brown)
Using a combination of the wet ingredient plus a dry ingredient will balance the texture.

Contents

Breakfast & Brunch

When it comes to gluten-free eating, breakfast and brunch foods can be off-limits. When I started cooking gluten-free, this was one of the first meals I tackled. I soon figured out that using one flour blend for almost everything made gluten-free cooking much less intimidating. But I also realized the taste and texture had to be right.

In this chapter, you will find your favorite breakfast and brunch recipes which I have converted to gluten-free: muffins, pancakes, waffles, doughnuts, crepes, quiche and more.

If you worry that baking is time-consuming, take advantage of down days, like the weekends, to make food ahead or mix the dry ingredients the day before. My kids are happy to eat reheated pancakes or waffles any morning. Remember, breakfast for dinner is always an option!

See the *Stocking the Pantry* and *Common Substitutions* chapters for more information on gluten-free ingredients, substitutions, and instructions for making *Amy's Gluten-Free Flour Blend*. Always check ingredients to make sure they are gluten-free.

⏱ *Time Saver Tip*

When you make a a batch of muffins, measure out another portion of the dry ingredients to store in a mason jar. Next time you want to bake them, you'll have your own muffin mix and will only need to measure the wet ingredients!

Pumpkin Muffin with Cinnamon Cream Cheese

Chef Tips

#1

For easy and consistent portioning, when making muffins, use a hinged-type ice cream scoop (also known as a scooper). These can be found at restaurant supply stores in different sizes.

#2

Always test muffins 1-2 minutes before the recommended time in case your oven is hotter than normal. Instead of using a tooth-pick to test for doneness, press your finger into the muffin. When it springs back, it's done. If it leaves an indentation, continue to bake and test in 1-2 minute intervals.

#3

Add ⅛ teaspoon of ground ginger to your muffin or quickbread mix; this helps to preserve the muffin's fresh-ness but will not affect the flavor.

When playgroup was being hosted at my house, I decided to make some blueberry muffins for the kids and moms. I wasn't sure how gluten-free would go over with a group of sometimes picky 2-year-olds. After seeing the batch devoured, I should have known back then I was on to something.

A good gluten-free muffin recipe needs two things: a blend of gluten-free flours and xanthan (or guar) gum. You can use the mix I suggest in the *Common Substitutions* section of the book (see Index), make your own, or buy a pre-made blend. If you use a pre-made blend and the results are less than perfect, please consider *Amy's Gluten-Free Flour Blend*. I find it perfect for almost everything.

Muffins can be varied into mini muffins or a loaf; see the temperature guidelines on the next page. Remember to store muffins in the fridge. If you don't use them in 2-3 days, put them in the freezer in an airtight bag.

"They were incredibly delicious! I LOVED the addition of the lemon. The lemon flavor really brightened the taste of the muffins." –tester

You can also substitute fresh, sliced strawberries or other whole berries for the blueberries.

Streusel Topping

4	tablespoons unsalted softened butter, cut into small pieces, or vegetable oil
¼	cup sugar or other natural sweetener
¼	cup *Amy's Gluten-Free Flour Blend*
¼	cup gluten-free rolled oats
¼	teaspoon kosher salt
½	teaspoon ground cinnamon

OPTIONAL INGREDIENTS:

¼	cup chopped nuts like walnuts or pecans

Mix all ingredients in a small bowl using your hands or a fork. Texture should be crumb-like. After muffins or loaf is portioned, place streusel mixture on top.

"Wow, they were so good! My kids loved them too, and said they were the best muffins in the world." –tester

Blueberry Muffins

2   cups *Amy's Gluten-Free Flour Blend*
2   teaspoons baking powder
½   teaspoon baking soda
½   teaspoon kosher salt
½   teaspoon xanthan gum
⅛   teaspoon ground ginger

2   large eggs
⅓   cup melted butter or vegetable oil
⅔   cup milk, yogurt, or milk substitute
½-¾ cup sugar or other natural sweetener
1   cup fresh (see note) or frozen
     blueberries (keep frozen
     until ready to use)

VARIATIONS: To make Blueberry Lemon muffins, add zest of one lemon and 2 tablespoons of lemon juice to the wet ingredients. You can substitute other berries like olallieberries, raspberries, or cut strawberries for the blueberries.

Note: if using fresh blueberries, make sure they are dry; otherwise they might sink to the bottom.

1. Preheat oven (see chart below) and get pans ready by either greasing them or using paper liners for the muffins.
2. In a large bowl, mix the dry ingredients (first 6 ingredients).
3. In a smaller bowl, mix the eggs. Add the butter or oil, milk, and sugar.
4. Add the wet ingredients to the dry ingredients and mix until combined. Mix the batter briskly for 5 seconds to help the batter to gel.
5. Fold in blueberries. Portion out muffins or loaf, filling about ⅔ full.
6. Use Baking Temps and Times Chart to determine baking time. See tips in the beginning of the Muffins and Loaves section to determine doneness.

Baking Temps and Times Chart

	Oven	Baking Time	Yield
REGULAR MUFFIN PAN	375° F	20-25 minutes	12-16 muffins
MINI MUFFIN PAN	375° F	15-18 minutes	40 mini muffins
LOAF PAN	350° F	35-40 minutes	1 loaf

Banana Muffins

2   cups *Amy's Gluten-Free Flour Blend*
2   teaspoons baking powder
½   teaspoon baking soda
½   teaspoon kosher salt
½   teaspoon xanthan gum
⅛   teaspoon ground ginger
½   teaspoon cinnamon

2   large eggs
⅓   cup melted butter or vegetable oil
⅔   cup milk or milk substitute
½-¾ cup sugar or other natural sweetener
1   teaspoon vanilla
2-3 ripe, mashed bananas

OPTIONAL INGREDIENTS (add to batter):
½ cup chopped nuts (walnuts or pecans)
½ cup shredded unsweetened coconut
½ cup semi-sweet chocolate chips

1. Preheat oven (see chart above) and get pans ready by either greasing them or using paper liners for the muffins.
2. In a large bowl, mix the dry ingredients (first 7 ingredients).
3. In a smaller bowl, mix the eggs, then add the butter or oil, milk, sugar, vanilla and banana.
4. Add the wet ingredients to the dry ingredients and mix until combined. Mix the batter briskly for 5 seconds to help the batter to gel.
5. Portion out muffins or loaf, filling about ⅔ full.
6. Use Baking Temps and Times Chart to determine baking time. See tips in the beginning of the Muffins and Loaves section to determine doneness.

Carrot Muffins

1¼ cups *Amy's Gluten-Free Flour Blend*
½ teaspoon baking powder
¾ teaspoon baking soda
1 teaspoon cinnamon
½ teaspoon kosher salt
½ teaspoon xanthan gum
⅛ teaspoon ground ginger

1 cup raisins
2 large eggs
½ cup melted butter or oil
¾-1 cup sugar or other natural sweetener
3 tablespoons water
1½ cups packed grated carrots
   (about 3-4 medium carrots)

OPTIONAL INGREDIENTS:
½ cup unsweetened shredded coconut
½ cup chopped nuts

VARIATIONS: To make Carrot-Zucchini muffins, substitute ½ of the amount of shredded carrots with shredded zucchini. To make Zucchini muffins, substitute shredded zucchini for carrot.

1. Preheat oven (see chart below) and get pans ready by either greasing them or using paper liners for the muffins.
2. In a large bowl, mix the dry ingredients (first 7 ingredients). Mix well then add raisins, making sure they are coated with flour.
3. In a medium bowl, add eggs and mix gently. Add butter or oil, sugar, and water. Mix well.
4. Mix flour mixture into wet ingredients, then add carrots. If using nuts and/or coconut, add with the carrots. Mix briskly for 5 seconds.
5. Pour batter into greased muffin tins, filling about 2/3 full. Place in oven.
6. Use Baking Temps and Times Chart to determine baking time. See tips in the beginning of the Muffins and Loaves section to determine doneness.

Baking Temps and Times Chart

	Oven	Baking Time	Yield
REGULAR MUFFIN PAN	375° F	20-25 minutes	12-16 muffins
MINI MUFFIN PAN	375° F	15-18 minutes	40 mini muffins
LOAF PAN	350° F	35-40 minutes	1 loaf

Pumpkin Muffins

This is a favorite muffin to bring to school for birthdays or treats. Even when I make it with low sugar, the kids still love it.

2 cups *Amy's Gluten-Free Flour Blend*
2 teaspoons baking powder
½ teaspoon baking soda
½ teaspoon kosher salt
½ teaspoon xanthan gum
1 rounded teaspoon ground cinnamon
½ teaspoon ground ginger
½ teaspoon ground nutmeg
¼ teaspoon ground cloves

2 large eggs
1 can (15 to 16 ounces) pumpkin puree
⅓ cup melted butter or vegetable oil
½ cup milk or milk substitute
½-¾ cup sugar or other natural sweetener
1 teaspoon vanilla

OPTIONAL INGREDIENTS:
½ cup chopped pecans
½ cup raisins

1. Preheat oven (see chart above) and get pans ready by either greasing them or using paper liners for the muffins.
2. In a large bowl, mix the dry ingredients (first 9 ingredients).
3. In a medium bowl, mix the eggs. Add the pumpkin, butter or oil, milk, sugar, and vanilla.
4. Add the wet ingredients to the dry ingredients and mix until combined. Mix the batter briskly for 5 seconds to help the batter to gel.
5. Portion out muffins or loaf, filling about 2/3 full. Place in oven.
6. Use Baking Temps and Times Chart to determine baking time. See tips in the beginning of the Muffins and Loaves section to determine doneness.

We were going to a kids' party and I knew my daughter would be faced with a buffet of off-limit food items. I made these carrot muffins for everyone, put a few aside for her, and soon the basket was empty. This recipe was my first real gluten-free success.

I love this picture of them eating the freshly shredded carrots. It's a true Family Chef moment!

Chef Tips

To make whole grain pancakes or waffles, substitute the *Amy's Gluten-Free Flour Blend* with an equal amount of another flour. For example, use 1 cup of the flour blend, ½ cup of gluten-free quick cooking oats or oat flour, ¼ cup of quinoa flour and ¼ cup of buckwheat flour.

You can also substitute the flour for other ingredients like ground nuts and cornmeal.

When making pancakes, a hot pan is key.

Making "Buttermilk"

Buttermilk that you see in the store is the sour liquid that is left after butter has been churned. It's great for baking and cooking, for both leavening and flavor. However, it can be difficult to find many uses for the leftover buttermilk. This is why it's sometimes easier to make your own version by simply adding an acid like vinegar or lemon to milk.

To make 1 cup of buttermilk, place 1 tablespoon of white vinegar or lemon juice in a glass measuring cup. Add milk or milk substitute to measure 1 cup. Allow to sit for 5 minutes. If you do this first before you measure the other ingredients, it will be ready when it's time to mix the batter.

Pancakes

2   cups *Amy's Gluten-Free Flour Blend*
2   teaspoons baking powder
1   teaspoon kosher salt
½   teaspoon xanthan gum
½   teaspoon cinnamon (optional)

1½   cups milk, milk substitute
     or buttermilk (see box
     on opposite page)
2   large eggs*
3   tablespoons sugar or other
     natural sweetener
3   tablespoons melted butter or
     vegetable oil
1   teaspoon vanilla

***To make pancakes extra fluffy, beat
the eggs with a whisk for 2-3 minutes**

This is a great starter recipe for pancakes. Making your own mix is very easy and economical. Do not make more than two times the recipes. Baking powder does not scale the same way the other ingredients do and it can give the batter a strange taste.

Makes twelve to fourteen 4" pancakes

1. In a medium bowl, mix dry ingredients (first 5 ingredients) with a whisk.
2. In a large bowl, beat egg briefly then add milk, oil, sugar and vanilla and mix.
3. Add dry ingredients to liquid ingredients, whisking together until there are no more lumps but without overmixing. Allow to rest for 5 minutes before using. Batter should be thin enough to pour. If it's not, add more milk or water.
4. While the batter is resting, place a non-stick griddle on the stove and heat to medium to medium-high or heat an electric to 425°F.
5. Once the griddle is hot, pour ½ cup of batter per pancake. When you see bubbles on top of the pancake, flip over and cook 2-3 more minutes. Pancakes should be golden in color.

Pumpkin Pancakes

2   cups *Amy's Gluten-Free Flour Blend*
2   teaspoons baking powder
1   teaspoon baking soda
½   teaspoon kosher salt
2   teaspoons cinnamon
½   teaspoon xanthan gum
¼   teaspoon nutmeg
¼   teaspoon ginger
¼   teaspoon ground cloves

1½   cups milk, milk substitute
     or buttermilk (see box
     on opposite page)
1   large egg*
3-4 tablespoons sugar or sweetener
1   cup pumpkin puree (not a full can)
2   tablespoons melted butter or
     vegetable oil
1   teaspoon vanilla

*See note above about eggs

You can make these pumpkin pancakes any time of the year. Pumpkin adds extra nutrition to this very popular breakfast dish.

Makes fourteen to sixteen 4" pancakes

1. In a medium bowl, mix dry ingredients (first 9 ingredients) with a whisk.
2. In a large bowl, beat egg briefly then add milk, sugar, pumpkin, oil, and vanilla and mix.
3. See step 3 above.
4. See step 4 above.
5. Once the griddle is hot, pour ½ cup of batter per pancake. Cook the first side for about 3-4 minutes or until the top just starts to bubble and begins to look dry. Then turn it over. The top should look medium-golden brown. Cook the second side for another 3-4 minutes.
6. The center of the pancakes should be fluffy. If it looks dense, cook longer.

Waffles

2¼ cups *Amy's Gluten-Free Flour Blend*
1 tablespoon baking powder
1 teaspoon kosher salt
1 teaspoon cinnamon

1¼ cups milk, milk substitute or buttermilk (see prior page)
3 tablespoons sugar or other natural sweetener
2 tablespoons melted butter or vegetable oil
2 large eggs
1 teaspoon vanilla

VARIATION: For whole grain waffles, use a combination of whole grain flours. See Chef Tips on previous page.

When making waffles, there are two important aspects; make sure you have some type of acid like buttermilk or yogurt and allow the batter to sit for 5 minutes before making waffles. Once you are familiar with the batter texture, you can really have fun. Whole grain, banana, pumpkin, chocolate chip, blueberry… make whatever you or your family likes. If you want to add puréed fruit like banana or pumpkin, add about ¾ cup and reduce egg to only 1.

Makes seven to eight 6" round waffles

1. In a bowl, mix flour, baking powder, salt and cinnamon.
2. In another bowl, combine milk, oil, sugar, eggs and vanilla. Slowly add dry ingredients to liquid ingredients, whisking together.
3. Allow to rest for 5 minutes before using. Batter will be thin; this makes it easier to pour. I usually use ½ cup of batter per waffle.
4. Follow waffle maker instructions. Carefully remove and serve. Cool before freezing.
Note: If you want crispier waffles, add more oil and/or cook longer.

French Toast

12-16 slices gluten-free bread

3 large eggs
⅔ cup milk or milk substitute
1 teaspoon vanilla
¼ teaspoon each cinnamon and nutmeg
Pinch or two of kosher salt

1 tablespoon vegetable oil (butter is tasty but burns too quickly in your pan; try this instead)

Chef Tip

Batter can be used immediately or saved for later. However, once bread is soaked, it needs to be cooked. Once it's cooked, it can be reheated in the microwave for 10-20 seconds.

This recipe is very straight forward. Make sure the bread is dry and that you work quickly; otherwise it will fall apart. You can use your favorite sandwich bread (cinnamon raisin works well) or use the recipes for White Bread or Cinnamon Raisin Bread (see Index).

Makes 6-8 servings

1. Toast bread slightly before using to dry it out. Allow to cool. If it's too soft, it will absorb too much batter and be mushy.
2. Mix all other ingredients except oil .
3. Heat a griddle or griddle pan to medium or grill pan to 400°F.
4. Based on the size of your pan, only batter the slices of bread that will be able to fit; don't let bread sit in the batter.
5. Place about ½ to 1 teaspoon of oil on pan and spread. Dip bread into batter and make sure it's coated well on all sides. Place bread on pan. Cook on each side until golden. Repeat with remaining bread. Keep warm in low temperature oven until ready to serve, covered with a damp paper or kitchen towel.

These waffles are so good, you'd be hard pressed to to tell that these aren't made with white flour. My son would eat them every day if I let him. Making homemade waffles serves other purposes besides a happy tummy. It is much more economical and usually less processed, depending upon the brand you buy.

"I made the French toast and it was delicious. I liked the tip about toasting bread first." —tester

Crepes

⅔ cup whole milk or milk substitute
⅓ cup cornstarch* or other starch
1 large egg
2 teaspoons olive oil or melted butter
Pinch of kosher salt

Olive oil for cooking

* To make a buckwheat style crepe, fill a ⅓ cup measure with equal amounts of cornstarch and buckwheat flour

Notes:

#1
Even though buckwheat has "wheat" in its name, it does not have gluten. However, due to potential cross-contamination issues, make sure the buckwheat is certified gluten-free if you are on a strict diet.

#2
For sweet crepes, fill with fresh fruit and confectioners' sugar, fresh squeezed lemon juice and sugar, Nutella, sliced bananas, or melted chocolate.

#3
For savory crepes, fill with shredded cheese, scrambled eggs, ham and cheese, sautéed mushrooms, shredded chicken with a thyme cream sauce, or spinach and cheese (see Index for tips on *Making Sauces*).

This recipe is based on one from Kate Chan who writes the blog, Gluten Free Gobsmacked. She has great recipes and is a wonderful writer. Whenever I make these, my kids get very excited. I have learned to make more than one recipe since these go quickly.

Makes 6 crepes in a 10" crepe pan (you can double this recipe to make more at once)

1. Place all ingredients in a blender and mix until combined. You can also mix well with a whisk.
2. Add a drizzle of oil to the pan. Heat crepe pan to just over medium heat. Making crepes is a little tricky so don't be surprised if the first one isn't perfect.
3. Lift the pan off of the heat and pour 3 tablespoons (1½ ounces) of batter or enough to cover the bottom of the pan while swirling the pan, off-heat, in a circular motion until the batter is covering the bottom without too many holes. Add a little more batter if necessary but do this quickly.
4. Cook for 20-40 seconds or until the edges are browned. You may also notice the edges will just start to pull away from the side. If the crepe is not brown, you may need to raise the heat.
5. Using a spatula, lift one edge of the crepe and then flip it over with the spatula, your fingers or tongs. Cook an additional 15-20 seconds. Remove and place on a plate.
6. Repeat with remaining batter, making sure to stir the batter in between as the cornstarch can settle to the bottom. Crepes are usually filled on one side, folded over and then folded again. See note to the left for filling ideas.

"I just made the crepes for lunch and they were delicious! Your recipe was true to every word, even the first crepe not turning out the best." –tester

If you don't have a crepe ladle, use a 2-ounce ladle filled to ¾.

Doughnuts

2½ cups *Amy's Gluten-Free Flour Blend* or 1½ cups white rice flour and 1 cup tapioca flour
1 teaspoon baking soda
½ teaspoon baking powder
1 teaspoon kosher salt
¾ teaspoon xanthan gum
½ teaspoon nutmeg

1 large egg, room temperature
½ cup sugar or other natural sweetener
1 cup plain yogurt or buttermilk, at room temperature (see Index about *Making Buttermilk*)
3 tablespoons unsalted butter, melted and cooled, or vegetable oil
1 teaspoon vanilla

VARIATION: for chocolate doughnuts, melt 3 ounces of unsweetened chocolate along with the butter and continue as directed.

Chef Tip

If you want more of a decadent and darker doughnut, bake the doughnuts for 7 minutes in the pan and cool slightly. Remove from the pan and place on a wire rack. Heat enough vegetable oil in a shallow pan to cover at least 1½". Cook doughnuts in hot oil for 40-60 seconds per side or until golden brown. Place on a plate with a paper towel to absorb the oil. Optionally roll in a mixture of white sugar and cinnamon.

This recipe is more reminiscent of an old fashioned or cake doughnut. The glazed-style usually has yeast which can be intimidating and time consuming. This is more like a muffin in a doughnut shape. However, by the look on the faces of these (non gluten-free) children, it doesn't seem to make a difference!

Makes 10-12 cake doughnuts

1. Preheat oven to 375°F for at least 15 minutes before; a hot oven is important.
2. Mix dry ingredients (first 6 ingredients) in a bowl with a whisk.
3. In another bowl, add the egg and beat for 1 minute. Add the sugar and mix for 30 seconds. Then add the yogurt or buttermilk, butter or oil, and vanilla. Mix until blended.
4. Add the wet to the dry and mix well. Give it one or two good mixes to "gel" the ingredients. Let the batter rest 10 minutes.
5. Place a pastry bag without a tip in a large drinking glass or jar and drape the top of the bag over the sides of the glass. This will make it easy to get the batter inside of the bag.
6. Grease the doughnut pan really well with butter or shortening; this will help with the browning.
7. Using a greased scooper or spatula, put about half of the batter into the pastry bag. Squeeze out batter into doughnut pan to make a circle. Fill all doughnut spaces. Spread lightly with your fingers or a greased spoon to smooth out. You can also transfer batter with a spoon; make sure to spread the batter.
8. Bake for 10-12 minutes or until doughnut springs back when you touch it. Remove from oven and let rest in pan for about 5 minutes. Remove and place on wire rack to cool.
9. Repeat with the next 6 doughnuts.
10. If you'd like, add a glaze (see right).

Even non gluten-free friends will enjoy these yummy doughnuts!

VANILLA GLAZE

Combine ½ to ¾ cup of confectioners' sugar, ¼ teaspoon of vanilla, and 1 to 2 teaspoons of milk or milk substitute to make glaze. Stir until all lumps are dissolved. Using a pastry brush, spread glaze over doughnuts.

MAPLE GLAZE

Follow the recipe above except substitute maple syrup or extract for the vanilla.

CHOCOLATE GLAZE

In a 2-cup glass measuring cup, place 2 tablespoons of unsalted butter and 2 ounces of bittersweet chocolate. Heat in the microwave in 30 second intervals until creamy and melted, stirring in between. You can also melt the chocolate in a small pot over the stove on low heat.

With a whisk, mix in ¾ to 1 cup of confectioners' sugar until smooth. Add 1 to 2 tablespoons of hot water, one tablespoon at a time, until the glaze is thin enough to pour but not too watery. Either dip the tops of the dough-nuts in the glaze or drizzle the glaze over the doughnuts. Optionally, add sprinkles.

"My son, 7, loved them and said he liked them more than our regular ones… Our non gf guest said 'Amazing! Perfect! Maybe more glaze.' He said they tasted even better with a glass of milk." –tester

Proofing The Yeast

Add yeast and sugar to warm milk. In about 5 minutes, the mixture should be foamy; this is called proofing the yeast (proving it's alive). If it's not foamy, you need to start over and use another packet.

Cinnamon Rolls

½ cup milk or milk substitute, between 105°F-115°F (warm but not hot)
1 packet (2¼ teaspoons) active dry yeast
1 teaspoon sugar

½ cup potato starch
1 cup corn starch
2 teaspoons baking powder
¼ teaspoon baking soda
1 teaspoon xanthan gum
½ teaspoon kosher salt

¼ cup + 1-2 tablespoons white sugar, separated
1 large egg, room temperature
¼ cup vegetable oil
2 tablespoons unsalted butter, melted and cooled (for dairy-free, use all oil)
1 teaspoon vanilla

OPTIONAL INGREDIENTS:
2 tablespoons *Amy's Gluten Free Flour Blend*

Filling
¼–⅓ cup brown sugar
¾-1 teaspoon cinnamon
OPTIONAL: ⅓ cup chopped nuts

Glaze
½–¾ cup powdered sugar
¼ teaspoon vanilla extract
1-2 teaspoons milk or milk substitute

VARIATIONS:
Orange: add 1-2 tablespoons of orange rind to the batter. Use 2 less tablespoons of milk and then add 2 tablespoons of orange juice to the egg and oil mixture.

Chocolate: Instead of cinnamon and sugar, add ½ cup chopped chocolate or chocolate chips as the filling.

OK, this falls into the category of a special treat but boy is it good. Read through the recipe first since there are a lot of steps. After you have made it once or twice, it will be much easier.

This recipe was adapted from the book "The Gluten Free Kitchen" by Robyn Ryberg.

Serves 6-8

1. Preheat oven to 375°F. Grease a 9" round baking dish.
2. Place warm milk in a glass measuring cup. Measure to just below the ½ cup mark, not above. Add the yeast and sugar to the milk and stir. See the note about proofing the yeast on the opposite page.
3. Mix dry ingredients (next 6 ingredients) in a small bowl.
4. In a medium to large bowl, add ¼ cup of sugar, egg, oil, butter, and vanilla. Mix well.
5. With a wooden spoon or plastic spatula, add the dry ingredients and yeast mixture to the wet ingredients and mix well, being sure to remove all lumps. Dough will be very soft. If the dough feels very sticky, mix in the other 2 tablespoons of gluten-free flour.
6. Place an 18" piece of plastic wrap on the counter. Sprinkle the remaining 1-2 tablespoons of white sugar evenly on the wrap. With a spatula, place the dough on the plastic wrap in the middle. Place another equally sized piece of plastic on top and press down with your hands until you have made a rectangle about 13-14" long.
7. Remove the top piece of plastic wrap. When you add the filling ingredients, leave about a 1" edge at the top so that the sugar does not spill out. Sprinkle the cinnamon all over the dough (use more if you like cinnamon). Next, sprinkle the brown sugar and nuts (if using) on top of dough evenly, pressing slightly.
8. As if you were rolling sushi, use the long piece of wrap to lift the edge of the dough closest to you and start to roll it up toward the edge furthest from you, forming a long cylinder. With a knife, cut the log into 1"-1½" slices and place into the pan. The dough will be very soft; do your best to get it into the pan without having the pieces break apart. You should have about 12-14 pieces. If you run out of room, place additional pieces in a small greased pan.
9. Bake 18-20 minutes, until the top is browned and crispy. If you like softer rolls, bake until just golden on top.
10. Mix glaze in a separate bowl. Drizzle glaze over warm rolls.

Granola is a great snack. It can be used with yogurt and fruit or even on top of vanilla ice cream. When you make your own, you save money and can control how much sugar and fat goes in. This oat-based snack can be packed with fiber, vitamins and nutrients and you can use whichever ingredients you like. Sweeteners add flavor to the mix while fat lends a crispiness. Nuts serve as a nice accompaniment along with the cinnamon and sunflower seeds.

For a healthy breakfast or snack, serve the granola with yogurt and fruit

Granola

4   cups gluten-free old-fashioned rolled oats
½   cup flax seeds
1½   teaspoons ground cinnamon
1½   teaspoons ground ginger
1   cup unsalted sunflower seeds
1   cup chopped walnuts or pecans
½   cup shredded unsweetened coconut

3   tablespoons molasses
2   tablespoons honey or maple syrup
⅓   cup sunflower or safflower oil
⅓   cup water

½   cup raisins
½   cup dried cranberries

Granola can be very expensive. Making your own with the ingredients you like and/or can tolerate seems like a good idea. Have you ever wondered how to make it? It's quite easy. All you need is the right ingredients, a big bowl and a rimmed sheet pan. That's it. Oh, I suppose a good recipe helps, too.

Makes 8 cups

1. Heat oven to 275° F. In a large mixing bowl, combine the oats, flax seeds, cinnamon, ginger, sunflower seeds, walnuts, and coconut.
2. Pour the molasses, honey or syrup, oil, and water over the mixture and stir until it is well coated. Spread evenly in one or two rimmed baking sheets.
3. Bake, stirring every 15 minutes, until dry and lightly browned—about 40 minutes. Let granola cool to room temperature, then add raisins and cranberries.
4. Store in an airtight container at room temperature for up to 1 month.

Grandma Rosie's Crustless Quiche

1 cup shredded or grated cheese (e.g. cheddar, mozzarella, Parmesan)
1 cup optional ingredients (see opposite page)

6 large eggs
2 cups milk or milk substitute (plain and unsweetened)
½ cup *Amy's Gluten-Free Flour Blend*
¾ teaspoon sea or kosher salt
¼ teaspoon ground pepper
¼ teaspoon nutmeg
¼ teaspoon dry mustard (or ½ teaspoon Dijon mustard)

This recipe can easily be cut in half to make fewer portions; simply use half of each of the ingredients

"It was SO good I think I ate 70% of it! Even my husband said, 'I don't like quiche but that was good.'" –tester

This is one of my signature recipes. I had been making it for years for brunches and parties. After the kids were born, it became part of the repertoire for birthday parties, playdates and easy meals.

Grandma Rosie used to make it with dry biscuit mix and a lot of olive oil. Over the years, I changed it by adding the milk and eliminating most of the mix. When we started eating gluten-free, I substituted the flour blend and it worked like a charm.

Serves 6-8

1. Preheat oven to 350° F.
2. Grease a 13" × 9" baking pan. Sprinkle cheese and about 1 cup total of any other ingredients in the bottom of pan. Omit cheese for dairy-free.
3. In a large bowl, whisk remaining ingredients. Pour egg mixture into pan. Place in oven and bake 30-40 minutes or until egg is set and top is golden brown and puffed.
4. Allow quiche to cool for at least 15 minutes before cutting.

You can also make this recipe in a cupcake pan for individual quiches, great for snacks and lunches.

Grease pan well with oil or a non-stick spray. Do not use liners. Bake for 20-25 minutes in a 375°F oven.

Flavor Variations

Place any of the following in bottom of pan before adding egg mixture.

Raw Vegetables: thin zucchini slices, halved cherry tomatoes or chopped tomato, chopped red pepper

Cooked Vegetables: par-boiled bite sized vegetables like asparagus, cauliflower, or broccoli; sautéed sliced onions, mushrooms, spinach, chard or kale

Cooked Meats: chopped cooked chicken, ham, sausage or crisp bacon, pancetta or prosciutto

Cheeses: goat, blue, feta, fontina, asiago, provolone, etc. Note: if using a salty cheese, reduce salt in the recipe to ½ of a teaspoon.

Quiche Lorraine Style: To the bottom of the pan, add 1-1½ cups cooked chopped bacon or ham, 1 cup shredded swiss cheese, and 1 sautéed, sliced onion.

1	box frozen, chopped spinach, thawed, drained and squeezed dry
½	cup crumbled feta
½	pint cherry tomatoes, halved, or ½ cup sun-dried tomatoes, chopped
6	large eggs
2	cups milk or milk substitute (plain and unsweetened)
½	cup *Amy's Gluten-Free Flour Blend*
½	teaspoon sea or kosher salt
¼	teaspoon ground pepper
¼	teaspoon nutmeg
½	teaspoon each dried oregano and garlic powder

SPINACH AND FETA CRUSTLESS QUICHE

Serves 6-8

1. Preheat oven to 350° F.
2. Grease a 13" × 9" baking pan. Add the following to the bottom of the pan: spinach, Feta, and tomatoes.
3. In a large bowl, whisk remaining ingredients. Pour egg mixture into pan. Place in oven and bake 30-40 minutes or until egg is set and top is golden brown and puffed.
4. Allow quiche to cool for at least 15 minutes before cutting.

Quiche

This recipe is one of those you don't whip up on a Tuesday morning but it is great for entertaining or on the weekends. It does take a lot of time but the results are fantastic. Make sure to read through the recipe as there is prep to be done beforehand.

Serves 6-8

CRUST

4	tablespoons unsalted butter, cut into ½" cubes
4	tablespoons vegetable shortening (you can use all butter or, for dairy-free, all shortening)
1¾	cups *Amy's Gluten-Free Flour Blend*
¾	teaspoon xanthan gum
½	teaspoon kosher salt
1	egg, lightly beaten
2	teaspoons white or apple cider vinegar
1-2	tablespoons ice water

QUICHE

6	large eggs
1½	cups half & half, cream, or milk substitute (plain and unsweetened)
1	cup shredded sharp cheese like cheddar, Swiss or Parmesan (or a combination of all)
½	teaspoon sea or kosher salt
⅛	teaspoon ground white pepper
⅛	teaspoon nutmeg

Filling such as ½-1 cup sautéed onion, par-cooked broccoli, chopped ham, crispy chopped bacon, etc. See prior page for more ideas.

You can use all butter if you don't have shortening but using the shortening makes the crust flaky. For dairy-free, use all shortening.

For more information about making the crust, see page 244, Chef Tips: Pie Crust.

MAKE CRUST

1. Place butter and shortening in a small bowl in the freezer to get extra cold. It only needs to be in there for 5 minutes. By the time you are done measuring the flours, it will be cold enough.
2. Place flours, xanthan gum, and salt into a food processor. Pulse a few times to mix. Alternatively, mix this in a medium bowl.
3. Add very cold shortening and butter to the processor. Pulse for 10-20 seconds or until shortening and butter is chopped. The mixture should look like grated Parmesan cheese. If you don't have a food processor, use a pastry blender to blend the butter and shortening with the flour mixture, or use two knifes to "cut" the shortening and butter into the flour mixture.
4. Remove butter and flour mixture and add to a medium sized bowl.
5. Mix the egg and vinegar in a small bowl. Add 1 tablespoon of the ice water, reserving the last tablespoon if needed. Add this to the butter and flour mixture, using your hands to mix. Dough should stick together well. If it doesn't, add a few drops of water until it does.
6. Shape dough into one large disc. Wrap in plastic wrap and place in fridge for at least 30 minutes or up to 2 days. Take the disc out 5 minutes before you are ready to roll.
7. Roll dough to 1/8" between 2 pieces of plastic. Place dough in a 9" deep pie pan and cut away extra dough, leaving a 1" border. Save extra dough for another use. Fold edges over and crimp to make a crust. Place in the fridge for 20 minutes to harden the dough. This minimizes the dough from shrinking too much when baked in the hot oven. When the pie shell is in the fridge, preheat the oven to 350°F.

MAKE QUICHE

8. In a medium sized bowl, mix the eggs, half and half, and seasonings.
9. After chilling the pie shell, place the cheese and fillings in the bottom. Pour the egg-cream mixture into the shell.
10. Bake for 35-40 minutes or until crust is golden and eggs are set.
11. Cool for at least 15 minutes before cutting. Be careful as the crust is fragile and can crumble.

Contents

Soups and Salads

When I think of a warm kitchen, I often picture a big pot of soup on the stove. The dishes in this chapter also include some lighter foods that you could make for lunch, dinner, a potluck, or dinner party.

Pre-made soups can contain flour as a thickener or the broth can contain gluten. Making your own is always a safe and delicious option. People sometimes tell me they can't make soup. If you don't cook it long enough or don't add the right seasonings, it can taste like "dishwater," a term my mom used to use. Soup is good as a starter, a meal, or even a snack. It's also very easy. Generally, the way I make it is the same: sauté the vegetables with seasonings, add broth and other pantry ingredients, bring to a boil, and simmer. You'll see a pattern from recipe to recipe. Once you learn how to make soup, it's so easy to change a few ingredients and have a new meal.

I wanted to add salads because you may find it necessary to make your own dressings. Gluten can be hidden in the least likely places. I've included some of my favorite salad recipes, too, including coleslaw and pasta salads. The type of gluten-free pasta you use for a salad will make a big difference. Find the brand and style you like and stick with it. Unfortunately, gluten-free pasta salads will only last 1-2 days, and then the texture will become rubbery. If you eat them when fresh, you probably won't be able to tell the difference. I've fooled many by bringing it to a party. You can too!

See the *Stocking the Pantry* and *Common Substitutions* chapters for more information on gluten-free ingredients, substitutions, and instructions for making *Amy's Gluten-Free Flour Blend*. Always check ingredients to make sure they are gluten-free.

Cooking Lesson

BASIC KNIFE SKILLS AND HOW TO CUT VEGETABLES

BASIC KNIFE SKILLS
- Use a sharp knife and a large cutting board.
- Make a flat edge by cutting the item in half so the item doesn't roll.
- Hold the food like a "claw" to keep it steady and watch your thumb.
- The closer the cuts, the smaller the chop.

HOW TO CUT VEGETABLES
Cut vegetables into uniform pieces so that the veggies cook at the same rate. Try to be quick so that prep doesn't seem like a chore but not so quick that the pieces are uneven. You don't have to be perfect.

ONION: Cut onion in half, from the root end to the other end. Cut the opposite end of the root on each piece. Keeping the root intact holds the onion together better. Remove skin. Place one half on the cutting board, flat side down. From the root end, make small, long cuts in the onion, from one side to the other. Cut onion in the other direction to chop.

CARROT: Peel carrots and cut ends off. Cut in half lengthwise to create a flat surface. Cut each half into 2 or 3 pieces, depending upon the size of the carrot and then cut each piece into strips. Hold 6 or 8 strips together and cut in the opposite direction to create a chop.

CELERY: Cut celery with ends cut off into 2 or 3 pieces. Cut each piece into strips. Hold 6 or 8 strips together and cut in the opposite direction.

OTHER VEGGIES: Use this method to chop peppers, potatoes and squash, etc.

CHOP VS DICE VS MINCE
The thinner the strips have been cut and the shorter the distance between the cut going in the other direction, the smaller the pieces will be. A chop is the biggest and a mince is the smallest; a dice is somewhere in between. If you are pureeing the soup after, don't worry too much about the size of the pieces.

The closer the cuts, the smaller the chop.
What you are cooking determines the size.

Cook like a Pro…

MIREPOIX (MEER-PWA) AND MISE EN PLACE (MEEZ-ON-PLAZ)

WHAT IS A MIREPOIX?

Mirepoix is a French term and, in its basic form, is a combination of chopped onions, celery and carrots. It's the base for many soups as well as stocks which are used for gravies and sauces. Try to keep these three vegetables on hand so that making a soup is a breeze any night of the week.

WHAT IS MISE EN PLACE?

Mise en place is another French term that means "everything in its place." The concept means that before you start cooking, you should have all of your ingredients out and ready to go. For example, the vegetables are cut, the spices are on the counter, the greens are washed, etc.

MISE EN PLACE IN MY KITCHEN

I interpret mise en place differently. When I cook at home, I put most of my ingredients on the counter. If I'm going to make a soup, I put the pot on the stove, take out the vegetables, and take out the necessary equipment like a knife, vegetable peeler, can opener, and cutting board.

Once all of the ingredients are out, I put the pot on the stove and turn the burner to medium. Next, I cut the onion. By the time the onion is cut, the pan is hot. I add some oil (about 2 teaspoons) and the onions. I give the onions a quick stir or shake and add herbs and/or spices. I step away from the stove and let the pan do the work. I cut the other vegetables from hardest to softest, adding them gradually. This way, I'm working in parallel.

If I have more time or want to be able to come home and cook, I prep all of the vegetables ahead of time. Honestly, the former is what I usually do.

Chef Tips

- Any of the soups in this section can be made in less than one hour. Split peas and lentils do not need to be soaked and cook very quickly.

- Almost any of these soup recipes taste even better with a drizzle of good quality extra virgin olive oil and some fresh grated Italian cheese like Parmesan or romano.

- Soup goes great with bread. For easy gluten-free bread recipes, check the Index.

- Read about *Making Sauces and Gravies* (see Index) to learn how to thicken soup.

- If you want a soup that has more liquid, add more broth (about one cup) or water. If you add water, add more salt to taste.

- Soup needs salt. Unless you have dietary restrictions, don't be shy. If soup doesn't have enough salt, it will taste like "dishwater" (my mom's description).

- Timing is everything. When cooking the vegetables, add salt after they have been cooking for awhile. If you add the salt too soon, the moisture from the vegetables will release and they will steam, not sauté . I usually add the salt when I add the garlic, right before I add the broth.

- If the vegetables look dry, instead of adding more oil, add just a pinch of salt. This will release a small amount of moisture.

- If a soup is getting too thick, place a cover on the pot.

- Make sure to use a big enough pot with a large surface area. If you try to make one of these recipes in a pot that is small, the vegetables won't caramelize properly which means it won't taste as good.

To ensure your soup is gluten-free, use only gluten-free pasta or grains. If you buy pre-made broth, look for a gluten-free brand.

Cooking Pasta, Rice, or Grains in Soup

ADD PRE-COOKED

(A) Add pre-cooked pasta, rice, or a grain (like quinoa) to the soup. Simmer 5 minutes or until heated through.

OR COOK IN THE SOUP

(B) Add extra broth or water and bring to a simmer. See guide below. For example, if you are adding 1 cup of pasta, add 2 cups of water or extra broth.

(C) Add dry pasta, rice, or grain to the soup. For 4 servings of soup, add ¾-1 cup of dry pasta, rice or a grain.

(D) Cook an additional 10-35 minutes (see guide below).

PASTA AND GRAIN COOKING TIMES

ITEM	RATIO OF LIQUID TO ITEM	ADDITIONAL TIME TO SIMMER
Gluten-Free Pasta	2:1	10 minutes
Rice	2:1	20 minutes
Brown Rice	2.5:1	35 minutes
Quinoa	2:1	15 minutes

Vegetarian Tip

If you eat a vegetarian diet, you can make any of these soups! For the bean soups, leave out the ham and use a vegetable broth. For the chicken soups, make them the same way but substitute 1 to 2 cups of small white beans for the chicken.

Chef Tip

To make a quick and fancy large crouton, use a cookie cutter or glass and cut a piece of sandwich bread. Toast in the toaster oven or regular oven. Add butter and a pinch of salt.

Chicken Broth

1   chicken carcass (or bones from breast, leg, and thigh)
2-3   teaspoons sea or kosher salt
8   black peppercorns (or ½ teaspoon ground pepper; broth will have specks)
2   carrots, washed and cut into 3-4 pieces
2   celery stalks, chopped into 3-4 pieces
½   onion, cut into 3 or 4 chunks
1-2   bay leaves (you can omit but it does give the broth a nice flavor)

Enough water to cover the chicken or about 12 cups

One way to make sure you have gluten-free broth is to make it yourself. It's not as hard as you might think. Give it a try. It's a wonderful base for soups and sauces.

Yield 3 quarts

Place all ingredients in a large stock pot on the stove and cover. Bring to a boil and then lower to a simmer, keeping covered. Cook about 2 hours. Taste and add more salt if necessary. Cool 15 minutes.
Pour through a mesh strainer. Once broth has cooled, it can be placed in a container and frozen to use another time. Otherwise, use within five days.

Note:
If you buy a pre-roasted chicken from the grocery store, check the ingredients to ensure there is no gluten.

Vegetable Broth

About 4-6 cups various chopped vegetables like onions, carrots, celery, broccoli, zucchini, mushrooms, etc.
1-2   tablespoons olive oil
½   teaspoon ground pepper
3   teaspoons sea or kosher salt, divided in half

Roasting the vegetables will yield a dark and rich broth, similar to a beef or chicken stock. You can also follow the instructions above to make a vegetable broth; just leave out the chicken.

Preheat oven to 400°F.
Toss all ingredients in a bowl with half of the salt. Place on a rimmed baking sheet and put in the oven. Bake until fully cooked and browned. Pour the vegetables into a pot and cover with water and remaining salt. Bring to a boil and then lower to a simmer. Cook about 30-45 minutes.
Strain vegetables. Taste broth and add more salt if necessary. Reserve broth and store in glass jar or plastic container. You can puree vegetables to make a soup as well.

How To Make It...
Easy as 1, 2, 3

SOUP

1 Sauté vegetables with seasonings.

2 Remove veggies and cook chicken in same pot.

3 Add other ingredients and simmer at least 20 minutes.

Chicken Noodle Soup
(QUICK AND EASY RECIPE)

3   teaspoons olive oil, divided
½   onion, diced
2-3   carrots, diced
1-2   celery stalks, diced
½   teaspoon dried thyme
½   teaspoon dried sage
¼   teaspoon ground pepper

2   boneless, skinless chicken
       breasts, about 1 pound, cut
       into ¼-½" cubes (see note)
½-1   teaspoon sea or kosher salt
1   garlic clove, minced (optional)
4-5   cups chicken broth
1   cup frozen peas and/or corn
1   cup dry gluten-free spaghetti or
       fettucine, broken in quarters

Note: you can use 2 cups of cooked, diced chicken instead of uncooked. Skip step 2 and add chicken with the broth in step 3.

Serves 3-4

1. Heat medium to large pot over medium heat. Add 2 teaspoons of oil, then onions, carrots, celery, and seasonings but not the salt. Without stirring too often, allow to cook until the onion is soft and lightly browned. Add salt and garlic, if using. Cook for one minute.

2. Remove veggies and place in bowl. Over medium heat, add the remaining teaspoon of oil and chicken and cook until golden brown, stirring only a few times. Add the veggies back to the pot.

3. Add chicken broth and simmer together for about 10-15 minutes.

4. Add 2 cups of water and bring back to a simmer. Add pasta and cook about 8 minutes. Test pasta for doneness.

5. Add frozen peas and/or corn and bring back to a simmer.

6. Taste and adjust, adding more seasonings, pepper or salt if necessary.

"So easy and quick like you say. We loved it, including my 4-year-old son." –tester

Chef Tip

See the steps on the opposite page. Notice the process is always the same when you make soup.

Try making your own chicken broth. See page 56 for recipe.

Hearty Chicken Stew

3 teaspoons olive oil, divided
½ onion, diced
2-3 carrots, diced
1-2 celery stalks, diced
½-1 teaspoon dried thyme
½-1 teaspoon dried sage
¼-½ teaspoon ground pepper
1 teaspoon sea or kosher salt

2 boneless, skinless chicken breasts, about 1 pound, cut into ¼-½" cubes (see note)
2 cups chicken broth
2 cups milk or milk substitute, plain and unsweetened

SLURRY
Mix ¼ cup cornstarch with ¼ cup cold water

1 cup peas and/or corn

Note: you can use 2 cups of cooked, diced chicken instead of uncooked. Skip step 2 and add chicken with the broth in step 3.

When I eat out, I always miss being able to order the chicken stew or pot pie since most recipes are made with flour. I created this recipe to replicate those flavors. Once you make it, you will be amazed at how easy and delicious this dish is. It is the epitome of a warm kitchen.

See vegetarian variation below.

Makes 4-6 servings

1. Heat medium to large pot over medium heat. Add 2 teaspoons of oil, then onions, carrots, celery, and seasonings but not the salt. Without stirring too often, allow to cook until the onion is soft and lightly browned. Add salt. Cook for one minute.
2. Remove veggies and place in bowl. Over medium heat, add the remaining teaspoon of oil and chicken and cook until golden brown, stirring only a few times. When chicken is cooked, add the veggies back to the pot.
3. Add chicken broth and milk and stir. Slowly bring broth and milk to a simmer in the pot.
4. Make the slurry in a small bowl or cup, making sure to stir right before you add it to the soup as the starch settles to the bottom. Slowly add half of the slurry to the pot, stirring. Simmer and continue cooking. If stew is not thick enough, slowly add more slurry. Make more slurry if necessary. If the stew is too thick, add more milk or broth. Make sure to stir the bottom and sides of the pot.
5. Taste and season with additional salt, pepper, sage, and thyme.
8. Add peas and corn or a small bag of frozen mixed vegetables. Simmer about 5 minutes or until all ingredients are hot.
9. Serve with cooked gluten-free pasta or rice.

Hearty Non-Chicken Stew

I have a lot of friends who are vegetarian so I'm used to coming up with alternatives for meat. Instead of using a chicken replacement, try white beans instead.

Follow the recipe above except substitute 2 15-ounce cans of drained, rinsed white beans (about 4 cups) for the cooked chicken. Use vegetable broth instead of chicken broth.
Make sure to taste the stew. Add more seasonings if it's bland.

You can use this Chicken Stew recipe for Chicken Pot Pie (see Index).

Black Bean Soup

2 teaspoons olive oil
½ onion, diced
2 carrots, peeled and diced
2 celery stalks, diced
¼ teaspoon ground pepper
½ teaspoon each cumin, coriander, and oregano
1 tablespoon mild chili powder
1 cup or 8 ounces chopped ham (optional)

2 cloves chopped garlic
½ teaspoon sea or kosher salt
2 cans black beans, drained and rinsed, or 4 cups cooked beans
1 quart chicken or vegetable broth

OPTIONAL INGREDIENTS:
1 15-ounce can diced tomatoes, undrained

TOPPINGS:
½ cup shredded cheddar, 2-3 tablespoons chopped cilantro, ½ cup sour cream, and crushed tortilla chips

I love to make this soup on cold nights when there is a chill in the air and I'm short on time. Testers and cooking class students find it easy and delicious.

Serves 3-4

1. Heat pot to medium first. Add oil, then add onion, carrot, celery, and seasonings (herbs and spices) but not the salt. Stir once and cook, stirring only occasionally, making sure the vegetables don't burn but that they are browning.
2. After a few minutes, add the ham and stir once. Continue cooking until ham is lightly browned and vegetables are golden and slightly softened.
3. Add garlic and salt and cook for 1 more minute.
4. Add beans and broth. If you want something more like chili, add diced tomatoes.
5. Simmer about 20-25 minutes. Top each bowl with cheddar, cilantro, sour cream, and tortilla strips.

Note:
Canned beans can contain hidden gluten due to cross contamination. Always check with the manufacturer if you have celiac disease or a severe intolerance.

White Bean Soup

(PASTA E FAGIOLI)

2 teaspoons olive oil
½ onion, diced
2 carrots, peeled and diced
2 celery stalks, diced
¼ teaspoon ground pepper
½ teaspoon each oregano and thyme
1 cup or 8 ounces chopped ham (optional)

2 cloves chopped garlic
½ teaspoon sea or kosher salt
1 quart chicken or vegetable broth
1 15-ounce can white beans (e.g. cannellini), drained and rinsed
1 15-ounce can diced tomatoes, undrained
1 cup dry gluten-free small pasta like shells or elbows

OPTIONAL INGREDIENTS:
½ cup chopped spinach or some type of leafy green, like chard or kale

TOPPINGS:
½ cup Parmesan cheese
1 tablespoon chopped fresh parsley or 2 tablespoons pesto (see Index)

"This soup was a hit! I added chopped kale at the end."
–tester

Serves 3-4

1. Heat pot to medium first. Add oil, then add onion, carrot, celery, and seasonings (herbs and spices) but not the salt. Stir once and cook, stirring only occasionally, making sure the vegetables don't burn but that they are browning.
2. After a few minutes, add the ham and stir once. Continue cooking until ham is lightly browned and vegetables are golden and slightly softened.
3. Add garlic and salt and cook for 1 more minute.
4. Add chicken broth, white beans, and diced tomatoes. Allow to simmer for at least 20 minutes. If you want the soup thicker and more like a stew, add 1 cup less water in the next step and cook another 10 minutes before adding the pasta.
5. To cook the pasta, add 2 cups of water to the soup and bring back to a simmer. Add pasta and cook for 10 more minutes. Cooking the pasta in the water helps to thicken the soup.
6. Add chopped spinach, if using, and cook another 2 minutes. Taste and adjust seasonings.
7. Top with grated Italian cheese, parsley and/or pesto.

Tip:

For easy prep, use frozen chopped spinach that is sold in a bag. Frozen chopped spinach in a box must be thawed first. Cut spinach pieces might be too big but can be used. You can always use raw chopped spinach; let it wilt in the hot soup for about 3 minutes.

Italian Lentil Soup

2	teaspoons olive oil
½	onion, diced
2	carrots, peeled and diced
2	celery stalks, peeled and diced
¼	teaspoon ground pepper
½	teaspoon each oregano and thyme
1	cup or 8 ounces chopped ham (optional)
2	cloves chopped garlic
½	teaspoon sea or kosher salt
1	quart chicken or vegetable broth plus 1 cup water
1	cup green lentils, rinsed
1	15-ounce can diced tomatoes, undrained
2	cups cooked or 1 cup dry gluten-free small pasta like little shells or elbows

OPTIONAL INGREDIENTS:

½	cup chopped spinach or some type of green, like chard or kale

TOPPINGS:

½	cup Parmesan cheese
1	tablespoon chopped fresh parsley or 2 tablespoons pesto (see Index)

This is yet another quick and easy soup which produces delicious results!

Serves 3-4

1. Heat pot to medium first. Add oil, then add onion, carrot, celery, and seasonings (herbs and spices) but not salt. Stir once and cook, stirring only occasionally, making sure the vegetables don't burn but that they are browning.
2. After a few minutes, add the ham and stir once. Continue cooking until ham is lightly browned and vegetables are golden and slightly softened.
3. Add garlic and salt and cook for 1 more minute.
4. Add broth, water, lentils, and diced tomatoes. Allow to simmer for about 30 minutes or until lentils are soft. If soup is becoming too thick, either add water, ½ cup at a time, or put a cover on the pot. If you want the soup thicker and more like a stew, add 1 cup less water in the next step and cook another 10 minutes before adding the pasta.
5. To cook the pasta, add 2 cups of water to the soup and bring back to a simmer. Add pasta and cook for 10 more minutes. Cooking the pasta in the water helps to thicken the soup.
6. Add chopped spinach, if using, and cook another 2 minutes. Taste and adjust seasonings.
7. Top with grated Italian cheese, parsley, and/or pesto.

Flavor Variation

Note:

Lentils from the bulk bin can be contaminated with gluten from other foods. If you are very sensitive, use lentils from a bag and check with the manufacturer to ensure the lentils are gluten-free.

INDIAN LENTIL SOUP

Replace oregano and thyme with ½ teaspoon or more of each: cumin, coriander, and turmeric. Omit ham, pasta, and toppings. Optionally add 1-2 cups of chopped cauliflower during last 10 minutes of cooking. Add 1 cup of frozen peas at the very end. Top with a dollop of plain yogurt to cool it down.

Optionally, serve with *Flour Tortillas* (see Index) or over basmati rice.

Corn Chowder

2 teaspoons olive oil
2 teaspoons unsalted butter (for dairy-free, omit butter and replace with olive oil)
½ medium onion, diced
¼ teaspoon ground pepper
1 teaspoon sea or kosher salt
1 russet potato, peeled and cubed (about 2 cups)
2 cups chicken or vegetable broth
2 cups whole milk or milk substitute, plain and unsweetened
3-4 cups corn (frozen or about 3 ears fresh)

SLURRY:
Mix 2 tablespoons cornstarch with 2 tablespoons cold water

OPTIONAL TOPPINGS:
Crisp, chopped bacon, shredded sharp cheddar, and/or chopped scallions or chives

This is a favorite recipe in our house. I make it all year round because frozen corn is prevalent and tasty. One tester said, "This chowder is delicious and super easy! My dad went on and on about it, saying it was the best corn chowder he'd ever had."

1. Over medium heat in a soup pot, add olive oil, butter, onion, pepper, and salt. Cook until the onion is soft.
2. Add the potatoes, broth, and milk. Bring to a boil, then lower to a simmer for about 5 minutes or until the potatoes are just starting to get soft but not mushy.
3. Add the corn. If using fresh corn, cook 5 minutes; if using frozen corn, cook 3 minutes. Check the potatoes to make sure they are soft but not mushy. Add the slurry and cook until thickened, about 3-5 minutes.
4. Taste and adjust seasonings if necessary.
5. Optionally garnish with crisp, chopped bacon, shredded sharp cheddar, and chopped scallions or chives.

Note:
If you use low or non-fat milk, or if you want a thicker chowder, use more slurry.

Clam Chowder

2 teaspoons olive oil
2 teaspoons unsalted butter (for dairy-free, omit butter and replace with olive oil)
½ medium onion, diced
1 stalk celery, diced
¼ teaspoon ground pepper
1 teaspoon sea or kosher salt
1 russet potato, peeled and cubed (about 2 cups)
2 cups whole milk or milk substitute, plain and unsweetened
1-2 6.5-ounce undrained cans of clams
1 8-10-ounce bottle of clam juice

SLURRY:
Mix 2 tablespoons cornstarch with 2 tablespoons cold water

Follow the directions above with the ingredients to the left.

Add the celery with the onions. Drain the clams and reserve juice. When you add the milk, add all of the clam juice (substitute chicken or vegetable broth if you can't find bottled clam juice). Substitute clams for the corn.

Optionally, garnish with chopped fresh parsley and plain gluten-free crackers or *Croutons* (see Index).

Caesar Salad

1-2 garlic cloves, cut in small pieces
½ cup regular mayonnaise
¼ cup grated Parmesan (or any hard Italian cheese)
2 tablespoons olive oil
1 teaspoon sea or kosher salt
Juice from ½ lemon
¼ teaspoon ground pepper

DRESSING

Makes about 1 cup or enough for 10-12 servings. Can be doubled.

Place all ingredients in a small food processor and pulse for 10-15 seconds. Process for 1 minute or until the garlic is chopped. Keep refrigerated until ready to use.

Toss with crisp, romaine lettuce, croutons, and optionally, shredded carrots.

DAIRY-FREE AND EGG-FREE VERSIONS

Follow directions above with the ingredients listed below. Taste and adjust seasonings if necessary. Since there is no cheese, you many need more salt.

DAIRY-FREE

1-2 garlic cloves, cut in small pieces
½ cup regular mayonnaise
2 tablespoons olive oil
1½ teaspoons sea or kosher salt
Juice from ½ lemon
½ teaspoon Dijon mustard
¼ teaspoon ground pepper

DAIRY-FREE AND EGG-FREE

1-2 garlic cloves, cut in small pieces
½ cup olive oil
1 teaspoon Dijon mustard
1½ teaspoons sea or kosher salt
Juice from ½ lemon
¼ teaspoon ground pepper

½ loaf of gluten-free baguette bread, cubed or 8 slices of gluten-free bread, cut into cubes

2-3 tablespoons olive oil

¼ teaspoon ground pepper
½ teaspoon each sea or kosher salt, oregano, and thyme

CROUTONS

If you want a crisper crouton, use more oil.

In a large bowl, toss bread cubes with olive oil and seasonings. Place on a rimmed baking sheet. Bake in a 400° F oven until brown and crisp, about 8-10 minutes.

Store covered at room temperature.

It's easy to make
your own croutons.

"Make in the Bowl" Dressings

SIMPLE VINAIGRETTE DRESSING

This isn't so much a recipe as a methodology. I like this dressing because I make it right in the salad bowl; no measuring and one less container to clean. The kids like it because it's a little sweet. Oh, and I like that they eat this salad!

In a bowl of mixed greens (about 3 cups) and/or vegetables, add:
2 teaspoons olive oil
½-1 teaspoon of rice wine vinegar (not rice wine) or
balsamic vinegar
A drizzle of agave nectar, maple syrup, or honey
Kosher salt and ground pepper to taste (few dashes of each)

Make it more Asian: Use rice wine vinegar. Add 1 teaspoon sesame oil, 1 clove fresh crushed garlic, and 1 teaspoon minced ginger (or ½ teaspoon garlic powder and ½ teaspoon ground ginger).
Make it Italian: Use balsamic vinegar. Add 1 minced garlic clove (or ½ teaspoon garlic powder) and ½ teaspoon dried oregano or basil. Top with 1-2 tablespoons grated Parmesan or Italian cheese.
Make it Greek: Use red wine vinegar in place of rice wine vinegar. Add 1 minced garlic clove (or ½ teaspoon garlic powder), and ½ teaspoon dried oregano. Top with feta cheese.

"I love this recipe! I can't stand bottled dressings. But making my own dressing is just enough of a hurdle that I wind up rarely making salads, except on special occasions. This method is so easy that I might just be making salads on a regular basis." –tester

Ranch Dip or Dressing

½ cup mayonnaise

1 cup yogurt, sour cream, or buttermilk (see the *Common Substitutions* chapter for tips on how to make buttermilk and/or how to substitute dairy)

1 teaspoon sea or kosher salt

¼-½ teaspoon garlic powder or granulated garlic

¼ teaspoon dry mustard or ½ teaspoon Dijon mustard

Scant ¼ teaspoon ground pepper

¼ teaspoon dry dill (or 1 teaspoon fresh, chopped)

1 tablespoon chopped fresh parsley

1-2 tablespoons milk or milk substitute (dressing only)

Ranch dressing is one of those items you would assume would be gluten-free until you look at the label. I normally don't make everything from scratch but here's one example of when it's worth it. Assuming you have the ingredients in your kitchen (which I usually do), this can be whipped up in less than 5 minutes. When I was testing the recipe, my son announced, "That's the best ranch dressing I ever had." OK, there's my motivation!

To make dip, mix all ingredients. Place in the fridge and wait at least 30 minutes before using.

To make dressing, mix all ingredients plus milk which will make it looser. Follow directions above.

VARIATION—BLUE CHEESE*

Omit parsley and dill from above. Add 4 ounces of crumbled blue cheese to make it into a dip. Add 1-2 tablespoons of milk to make it into a dressing.

*Most blue cheese is gluten-free, even when the mold is started on bread. However, always check with the manufacturer.

"Oh, Amy, you have transported me again! This time, to my first cooking lesson in my grandmother's kitchen as a child. She taught me how to make ranch dressing, which I have loved ever since." –tester

Chef Tips

Are you tired of throwing out salad because you use too much lettuce? Waste less by using this measurement; one handful of lettuce per person plus one "for the bowl" (i.e. one extra handful). If you have big salad eaters, use one and a half handfuls per person. It works perfectly almost every time!

In almost every class, I am asked which type of olive oil to use. Cook with generic, less costly extra virgin olive oil and use the more expensive, smoother, spicier olive oil for salad dressings like these.

All-American Macaroni Salad

1   pound gluten-free elbow or small pasta

1   cup regular mayonnaise
1-2 tablespoons white vinegar
½   medium diced white or red onion (see note)
1-2 medium celery stalks, diced
2-3 hard boiled eggs, chopped (see directions on opposite page)
1   teaspoon sea or kosher salt
¼   teaspoon ground pepper
1   tablespoon yellow mustard

OPTIONAL INGREDIENTS:
1   small can of chopped black olives, drained, and/or ½ cup of shredded carrots.

I don't know about you but eating macaroni salad makes me feel "normal." How many picnics or potlucks have you been to where you have to pass on this dish? This recipe is a simple American macaroni salad.

Serves 6-8

1. Cook pasta; see *Gluten-Free Pasta Cooking Tips* for tips (see Index). Pasta should be somewhat firm, but not mushy.
2. While the pasta is cooking, prep the other ingredients and place in a large bowl.
3. Once pasta is cooked, drain and rinse with cold water. Pasta should still be a little wet/loose. Make sure to not wait too long before mixing with the other ingredients; otherwise it will be difficult to stir.
4. Add pasta to the bowl and mix gently, using care not to over-mix. Macaroni salad will be a little loose before being chilled. After it chills, it will be the correct texture.
5. Chill for at least one hour. Before serving, stir and taste for seasonings, adding more salt, mustard, or vinegar if it tastes "flat."

Creamy Coleslaw

8   ounces shredded cabbage (about ½ head or 4 cups)
1-1½ cups shredded carrots (about 2-3)

Dressing:
⅓   cup regular mayonnaise (or vegan mayonnaise for egg-free)
¼   cup sour cream (see *Common Substitutions* chapter for a dairy-free option)
¾   teaspoon sea or kosher salt
¼   teaspoon white pepper
1   tablespoon agave nectar or honey
1   tablespoon apple cider vinegar
1   teaspoon Dijon mustard or ½ teaspoon dry mustard

It's easy to whip up this simple salad to serve for lunch or parties. It's another recipe that is very flexible; you can use a little less or use a little more of the cabbage or carrot. To make it tangier, add an extra teaspoon (or more) of vinegar and mustard.

Serves 4-6

Combine all dressing ingredients in a large bowl. Add cabbage and carrots. Chill for at least one hour.

Tip:

Try adding *Peanut Sauce* (see Index) instead of the creamy dressing to the cabbage and carrots for an Asian-flavored slaw.

Chef Tips

Gluten-free pasta salad doesn't keep that well (the pasta can become rubbery) so if you don't think a full recipe will be eaten in two days, cut this in half.

To make onions less harsh-tasting, soak chopped onion in ice water for 5 minutes. Drain and add to recipe. Optionally, omit the onion.

For an egg and dairy-free coleslaw or macaroni salad, use a soy-based mayonnaise for the mayo and sour cream.

Cooking Perfect Hard Boiled Eggs

This recipe is so easy. It works for me every time.

1. Place room temperature eggs in a pot large enough to hold them in single layer. Add cold water to cover eggs by 1". Heat over high heat just to boiling. Remove from burner. Cover pan.
2. Leave eggs in hot water about 12 minutes for large eggs (9 minutes for medium eggs; 15 minutes for extra large).
3. Drain immediately and cool completely under cold running water or in a bowl of ice water. Refrigerate.
4. Peel once eggs are completely cooled.

"It was pretty quick to make and could be served warm or cold. I like to make the next day's meal right after we eat. That way food is ready when I come home from work." –tester

Thai Peanut Noodle Salad

8-12 ounces gluten free noodles like spaghetti, linguine, or buckwheat noodles, broken in 3" pieces

8   baby carrots or 2 peeled carrots, chopped, or 1 cup shredded carrots

½   cup peanuts, chopped (see note)

8   ounces firm tofu, cubed in small pieces (you can also use cooked, chopped chicken or shrimp)

1-2   scallions, chopped, white and green parts

1   tablespoon cilantro, chopped

1-2   tablespoons sesame seeds

1   cup Peanut Sauce (see Index)

OPTIONAL INGREDIENTS:
To make spicier, add a few dashes of cayenne pepper or chili oil in step 5.

NOTE:
You can use cashews instead of peanuts for the above and cashew butter instead of peanut butter in the peanut sauce recipe.

When I brought this dish to a barbecue, I didn't tell anyone it was gluten-free; I just put it on the table and made sure the hostess knew it had peanuts. When we got to the table to get our lunch, it was almost all gone! Of course, using good ingredients like cilantro and natural peanut butter really helps to make the dish flavorful. Use what you have, and this salad will be a big hit. One tester added shrimp to make it a meal. Another suggested adding more crunchy vegetables like chopped cucumber, celery, green pepper, or shredded Napa cabbage. Add up to ½ cup of any of these.

Serves 4-6

1. Cook pasta; see *Gluten-Free Pasta Cooking Tips* for tips (see Index). Pasta should be somewhat firm, but not mushy.
2. While the pasta is cooking, prep the other ingredients.
3. In a small sauté pan, toast sesame seeds without oil over medium heat, being careful not to burn them. After the seeds are toasted, place in a bowl to cool.
4. Once pasta is cooked, drain and rinse with cold water.
5. Gently toss all ingredients together in a large bowl. Taste for flavoring.
6. Refrigerate until ready to serve.

Contents

Main Dishes

I remember when I found out I needed to give my daughter a gluten-free diet; my reaction was, "All I know how to make is pizza, pasta, bread, and cookies. What am I going to do?" Once I got over my shock, I started experimenting with different dishes and, of course, pastas. Now that we all eat gluten-free, it's not really a big deal anymore.

When it comes to main courses, there are plenty of dishes that naturally do not contain gluten like grilled and roasted meats, stir fried veggies with rice, and any rice or potato-based dish. But you might want that "warm kitchen" feeling with dishes like pasta and traditional comfort foods. This is the chapter for you.

Almost all of the recipes in this chapter are for dishes which traditionally use gluten like the pastas, pot pie and meatballs, but there are some others which are naturally gluten-free as well.

All of these are recipes I make for my family and /or prepare in my cooking classes. Eating gluten-free has forced us to get out of the pizza-pasta-bread with dinner routine. It's not to say you can't have these dishes; only that it has been a good thing to vary our diet. For that, I am grateful.

See the *Stocking the Pantry* and *Common Substitutions* chapters for more information on gluten-free ingredients, substitutions, and instructions for making *Amy's Gluten-Free Flour Blend*. Always check ingredients to make sure they are gluten-free.

Sauces and Gravies

I think sauces were the first thing I learned to make in culinary school. To me, a sauce is what can differentiate a good dish and a great dish. It's the quintessential item to learn in school, and valued by chefs, regardless of where they are from. Learning some basic sauces (gravy, white, and tomato, as well as a basic pesto) can propel your home cooking from so-so to my-oh-my. When I think of a warm kitchen, it often includes a sauce.

I make sauces all of the time to give food extra flavor and moisture. Sauces can compliment and even enhance your dishes, especially those made in a pan. However, sauces are often prepared with flour. Welcome to the world of gluten-free sauces and meet your new best friend, "the slurry."

Don't think you have to be a culinary master to "master" these techniques.

Definitions: Types of Sauces

BASIC SAUCE OR GRAVY Don't think of making sauce or gravy just at Thanksgiving; it can be made all year round. This sauce can be served over meat, rice, or pasta.

WHITE SAUCE OR BÉCHAMEL You might see this on a restaurant menu as it is a great base to many dishes. You can vary the type of milk that you use depending upon how much fat you want in the dish or what's in the fridge. If you have a dairy intolerance, use a butter substitute or plain coconut oil instead of butter and any plain, unsweetened milk substitute to replace the milk. What's great about a béchamel sauce is that it is the base for many other sauces and dishes like *Mac and Cheese and Hearty Chicken Stew* (see Index).

PAN SAUCES When I used to sauté vegetables or meat in a pan in some fat, I would add flour to the pan to make a sauce. Now, I add the liquid first and use a slurry to thicken the sauce. The flavors that develop in a pan are marvelous, and this is an easy way to not only capture those but not have to dirty another pan. Pan sauces can be used in pasta or rice dishes and for entrees like *Shepherd's Pie* (see Index).

TOMATO SAUCE I hope my mom doesn't mind, but I'm giving you the family recipe. I haven't met anyone who doesn't like this quick, fresh, and tasty sauce. The recipe for bolognese or meat sauce is a variation of that one. It is delicious with pasta or can be used for *Cheese Lasagna* (see Index). Besides the family sauce recipe, there is also another, even simpler, tomato sauce, which I learned while in Italy.

PESTO SAUCE There are many types of pesto; basil pesto is the most popular. Traditionally, it is made from fresh basil and some other pantry ingredients. Add the ingredients to your food processor and in about 5 minutes, you can create a delicious pesto. I'm surprised that many children like this even though it's green. It's great on pasta, a sandwich or can be added to tomato sauce if you are out of basil. It can even be made dairy-free.

Chef Tips

Instead of a flour-based roux, use a slurry to thicken anything like sauces, soups, and gravies.

1

2

3

How To Make It...
Easy as 1, 2, 3

BASIC SAUCE OR GRAVY

1 Bring liquid to a simmer

2 Add slurry and stir sauce with a whisk

3 Continue to cook, stirring occasionally, until thickened and the starchy texture is gone

📖 Cooking Lesson

Making Sauces and Gravies

1 **cup broth of choice (e.g. chicken, vegetable, or beef broth)**

SLURRY:
Mix 1 tablespoon cornstarch with 1 tablespoon cold water

SEASONINGS:
¼-½ teaspoon sea or kosher salt
⅛ **teaspoon ground pepper**

OPTIONAL INGREDIENTS:
1 **tablespoon unsalted butter or butter substitute**

SIMPLE GRAVY TO SERVE WITH CHICKEN, VEGETABLES, BEEF, OR PORK

Makes 4 servings; to make more, scale proportionately

1. Heat broth in a small to medium sized pot to a simmer.
2. Meanwhile, make the slurry by mixing the water with starch in a small bowl. Mix until smooth and the slurry looks like whole milk.
3. Add slurry to heated broth and stir with a whisk. Season with salt and pepper. Add more salt to taste, especially if you are using a low-sodium broth.
4. Simmer 4-6 minutes or until thickened. If the sauce is not thick enough, make and add more slurry. Add butter at the end to make the sauce more creamy and similar to a roux-thickened sauce.
5. Taste the sauce to make sure the starch is cooked. If there is a gritty texture, the sauce needs to cook more.

Variations

For variations, add the following ingredients to the sauce in the first step. You may need to add more slurry to achieve the proper thickness.
LEMON AND GARLIC: Add 1 teaspoon lemon juice and 1 minced garlic clove to a chicken or vegetable broth. Simmer at least 2 minutes.
WINE AND HERB: Add 2 tablespoons of dry white wine and 1 teaspoon of dried herbs to the broth.
MUSTARD: Whisk in 1-2 teaspoons Dijon or grainy mustard into the sauce as it thickens.
CREAMY: Add 1 tablespoon cream to any of the above variations. For dairy-free, use any plain and unsweetened milk like soy, coconut or almond.

How to Make a Slurry:

For every cup of liquid, add a slurry:

1 **tablespoon of a starch (cornstarch, potato starch, arrowroot, or tapioca)**

mixed with

1 **tablespoon of cold water**

Basic White or "Cream" Sauce

TO SERVE WITH VEGGIES, PASTA, CHICKEN, PORK, SHRIMP, OR RICE

Makes 4 servings; to make more, scale proportionately

1 cup milk or milk substitute, plain and unsweetened

SLURRY:
Mix 1 tablespoon cornstarch with 1 tablespoon cold water

SEASONINGS:
¼-½ teaspoon sea or kosher salt
⅛ teaspoon ground pepper
Sprinkle of nutmeg

OPTIONAL INGREDIENTS:
1 bay leaf (for flavor)
1 tablespoon unsalted butter or butter substitute (for texture)

1. Heat milk to a simmer in a small to medium sized pot, making sure milk is not boiling.
2. Meanwhile, make the slurry by mixing the water with starch in a small bowl. Mix until smooth and the slurry looks like whole milk.
3. Add slurry to heated milk and stir. Season with salt, pepper, nutmeg, and the bay leaf, if using. Add more salt to taste or if you are using a low-sodium broth.
4. Simmer 4-6 minutes or until thickened. If the sauce is not thick enough, make and add more slurry. Add butter at the end to make the sauce more creamy and similar to a roux-thickened sauce.
5. Taste the sauce to make sure the starch is cooked. If there is a gritty texture, the sauce needs to cook more.

Variations

For variations, add the following ingredients to the recipe above in the first step. You may need to add more slurry to achieve the proper thickness.

LEMON AND GARLIC CREAM: Add 1 teaspoon lemon juice and 1 minced garlic clove to the milk. Simmer at least 2 minutes.
CREAMY WINE AND HERB: Add 2 tablespoons of dry white wine and 1 teaspoon of dried herbs to the milk.
CREAMY MUSTARD: Whisk in 1-2 teaspoons Dijon or grainy mustard into the sauce as it thickens.
PESTO CREAM: Add 1 tablespoon of *Basil Pesto* (see Index) to the milk.
MUSHROOM CREAM: See Index for *Wild Mushroom Marsala Sauce* variation.

Chef Tip

A white sauce can be used as the base for many other sauces which can be added to vegetables, proteins, or pasta. See the Variations to the right for instructions.

How to Make It…
Easy as 1, 2, 3

ALFREDO SAUCE

1 Make the cream sauce following the directions to the left and add ⅛ teaspoon garlic powder or granulated garlic and 2 more pinches of ground pepper to the milk.

2 When the sauce has thickened, shut off heat and add ½ cup grated sharp Italian cheese (e.g. Parmesan or pecorino) and stir. After 5 minutes, stir again. If the cheese has not melted, reheat the sauce for a few minutes. Taste and adjust seasonings. To make it extra creamy, add 1-2 tablespoons of heavy cream.

3 Serve with 2-3 cups of cooked pasta.

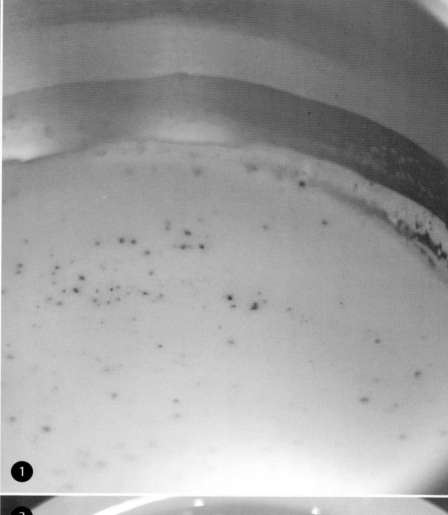

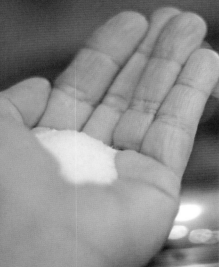

Cooking Pasta

You may not think you need instruction on how to cook pasta but gluten-free pasta is not as straightforward as regular pasta. Many people think it is not palatable, but so much has to do with how it's cooked. If you are not satisfied with the texture of gluten-free pasta, try these tips.

GLUTEN-FREE PASTA COOKING TIPS

• Pasta doubles when it cooks. 1 cup of dry pasta will create 2 cups cooked pasta.

• Make sure there is plenty of water when cooking pasta. Use a stock pot not a sauce pan. A large amount of water ensures that the pasta cooks evenly and does not stick. Don't add oil; it's a waste of money.

• Use a cover to bring the water to a boil quickly and most efficiently.

• Italians add a lot of salt to the boiling water when they cook pasta. I've come to use almost a tablespoon when I'm cooking a pound of pasta. However, be careful when you add the salt because the water might spit a bit and burn you. It flavors the pasta and helps it to be absorbed better by the sauce.

• Once you add the pasta to the water, stir the pasta with a large spoon or fork. Continue to stir every 2-3 minutes or the pasta may stick to the bottom of the pan. Stay near the stove and use a timer for cooking.

• Test pasta after about 8 minutes, regardless of what the package says (test after less time if the pasta is small). If it's not done, continue to test in 1-2 minute increments until pasta is cooked to your liking.

• Only rinse pasta with water if you are going to be serving it cold in a salad. Otherwise, drain, shake, and then add the sauce.

• Once cooked, don't over-stir or the pasta will break apart.

SAUCES FOR PASTA

Now that you know how to cook your pasta perfectly, start experimenting with some of my best sauces. See Index for recipes below:

* Weeknight Tomato or So Simple Tomato sauce
* Bolognese sauce
* Pesto sauce (basil or sun-dried tomato)
* Cheese sauce
* Alfredo sauce
* Mushroom cream sauce

USE THESE PASTA SHAPES WITH THESE SAUCES (SEE INDEX FOR RECIPES)

CAPELLINI/ANGEL HAIR

Butter, oil, *Basic Cream*, *Pesto*, *Weeknight Tomato*, *So Simple Tomato*.

FETTUCINE, SPAGHETTI, OR LINGUINE

Butter, oil, *Basic Cream*, *Alfredo*, *Meat*, *Weeknight Tomato*, *So Simple Tomato*.

PENNE, ROTINI, OR FUSILI

Butter, oil, *Basic Cream*, *Alfredo*, *Meat*, *Weeknight Tomato*, *So Simple Tomato*, pasta salad.

ELBOW AND DITALINI

Mac and Cheese, soups, pasta salad.

Chef Tips

For added nutrition (and one less pot to wash), add fresh or frozen vegetables to the boiling water of the pasta during the last two minutes of cooking. If you add a frozen vegetable, for example spinach, it might extend the cooking time a little as the frozen spinach will drop the temperature of the water. Ideas are: broccoli, cauliflower, peas, spinach, zucchini, shredded carrots, and chopped chard.

Mac and Cheese

**1½-2 cups gluten-free pasta
(shells or elbows)**
1   cup milk or half and half

SLURRY
**Mix 1 tablespoon cornstarch with
1 tablespoon cold water**

Sprinkle of nutmeg
½   teaspoon sea or kosher salt
**Few grinds of black pepper or a
sprinkle of white pepper**
**Sprinkle of dry mustard and garlic
powder**
¾   cup of shredded cheese*

***I use a combination of sharp cheddar,
Parmesan and a shredded Italian blend
that you might use for pizza. Using a
sharp cheese is important for flavor.
If your children are less than enthusiastic,
try the next recipe for a mild version.**

Making macaroni and cheese from scratch is not hard. Sometimes I make the cheese sauce in the microwave in a 2-cup glass measuring cup. Make it once or twice, and you'll quickly get the hang of it.

Serves 3-4

1. Bring a medium pot of water to a boil.
2. While you are waiting for the water to come to a boil, make the sauce. Add the milk to a small saucepan over medium heat. Heat until it is hot but not boiling. It is ready when there are little bubbles on the edges of the pot, also known as scalding.
3. When milk is hot, add cornstarch slurry and whisk. Add nutmeg, salt, pepper, mustard, and garlic. Continue to cook until slightly thickened, about 3-5 minutes. You might need to raise the temperature slightly.
4. When the water comes to a boil, add pasta and stir. See Index for *Gluten-Free Pasta Cooking Tips*.
5. Once the milk sauce has thickened slightly, turn off heat. Add cheeses and stir. Let the cheese melt for a few minutes and then stir. Set aside.
6. Once pasta is done, drain it and add back to pan. Add cheese sauce and stir to combine. Serve immediately.

Dairy Free Macaroni and "Cheese"

Just in case you can't eat dairy, here's an alternative to the sauce. It's not made from cheese, and it's a good alternative. If you like the taste and texture of alternative cheese, (like rice or soy), try adding these at the end.

Serves 3-4

1 **cup milk substitute, plain and unsweetened (soy milk is a very good substitute)**
⅛ **teaspoon each ground mustard, ground black pepper, and nutmeg**
Pinch or two of turmeric (for color)
¼-½ **teaspoon sea or kosher salt**

SLURRY
Mix 1 tablespoon cornstarch with 1 tablespoon cold water

1 **cup dry gluten-free pasta (shells or elbows)**

½ **cup cheddar cheese substitute (like Daiya®)**

1. Bring a medium pot of water to a boil.
2. While you are waiting for the water to come to a boil, make the sauce. Place the milk substitute in a small sauce pan over medium heat. Add seasonings, turmeric, and salt. Heat until it is hot but not boiling.
3. Once the milk substitute is hot, add slurry and whisk. Continue to cook until slightly thickened, about 3-5 minutes. You might need to raise the temperature slightly. Once the sauce has thickened slightly, turn off heat.
4. Add cheese substitute and stir. Set aside.
5. When the water comes to a boil, add pasta and stir. See Index for *Gluten-Free Pasta Cooking Tips*.
6. Drain pasta and place back in pot. Add sauce to pan and stir. Adjust seasonings if necessary.

Basic Cheese Sauce

If your family likes a simple cheese sauce, this is the recipe for you. It's tasty and easy. Serve this sauce over pasta, vegetables, or chicken. Use this sauce and follow the instructions on the previous page for cooking the pasta.

Makes 1½ cups sauce, enough for 4-6 servings

¾ **cup shredded mild cheddar cheese, not sharp**
1 **tablespoon cornstarch**

1 **cup whole milk or half and half**
½ **teaspoon sea or kosher salt**
Pinch of ground black or white pepper
1 **tablespoon unsalted butter**

1. In a small bowl, mix cheese with cornstarch so that the cheese is coated with the starch. Set aside.
2. Slowly heat milk or cream in a medium sized pot. Add seasonings.
3. When milk is starting to form bubbles on the sides (i.e., scalding), add the cheese, and lower the heat. Cook until thickened, about 3 minutes. Add more milk if it's too thick, 1 tablespoon at a time.
4. Add butter, stir, and taste. Adjust for seasonings. Add to pasta or vegetables.

Wild Mushroom Marsala Sauce

TO SERVE OVER MEATS, POLENTA, CROSTINI, PASTA

Using wild mushrooms gives this dish almost a meaty quality to it. My son has mistaken shitake mushrooms for chicken when it's in this sauce. This is my stand-by method for cooking mushrooms for any dish. If you don't like Marsala, simply omit from the recipe. You can substitute with white wine but not red; the red will make the sauce pink. This dish takes at least 20 minutes to prepare but is worth the effort.

Serves 4-6

1. Heat large sauté pan over medium heat. Add oil and only 2 teaspoons of the butter, then onion, herbs, and ground pepper. Do not add the salt yet. Cook, stirring once or twice, until golden and translucent.
2. Once softened, add the thicker/heartier mushrooms first like portobello or oyster. Stir once. Raise heat slightly and cook, stirring only occasionally until mushrooms become brown. If mushrooms are very dry, add a sprinkle of salt. Continue to add the mushrooms in batches until all of the mushrooms are cooked and brown. There should not be a lot of liquid in the pan; if there is, raise the heat to try to cook off the liquid.
3. Add salt and garlic and cook for 1-2 minutes, stirring.
4. Add Marsala and allow to cook for 1 minute or until mostly evaporated.
5. Add broth and stir. Bring to a simmer.
6. Make the slurry in a small bowl. Stir the slurry right before and then add to the pan. Stir to combine. Simmer until thickened, stirring occasionally. If sauce is not thick enough, make more slurry and add. Cook for 3-5 minutes.
7. Taste sauce before serving. Add more seasonings if it is bland. Add butter or butter substitute to give the sauce a creamier consistency.

Variations

MUSHROOM CREAM SAUCE
Substitute 1 cup of milk or milk substitute, plain and unsweetened, for 1 cup of the broth.

SAUTÉED MUSHROOMS
To make delicious sautéed mushrooms without the sauce, stop after step 4. Optionally, add 1 tablespoon of unsalted butter at the end.

2	teaspoons olive oil
1-2	tablespoons unsalted butter
1	medium onion, chopped
½	teaspoon herbs de Provence
¼	teaspoon ground pepper
1-2	pounds assorted mushrooms, sliced (portobello, crimini, shitake, white, oyster, porcini)
1	teaspoon sea or kosher salt
1-2	garlic cloves, minced
¼	cup sweet Marsala wine
2	cups chicken or vegetable broth

SLURRY
Mix ¼ cup cornstarch with ¼ cup cold water

OPTIONAL INGREDIENTS:
1 tablespoon unsalted butter

Chef Tips

If mushrooms look dry while cooking, resist the temptation to add more oil or butter. Try adding a pinch of salt to bring out enough moisture so that they don't dry out.

If you want deep brown mushrooms that are full of flavor and not grey and watery, add the mushrooms to the pan in batches. Then, add the garlic and salt right before the liquid is added. Salt draws out the moisture. Garlic will burn if added too early.

You can add ½ cup of chopped walnuts at the end to give the sauce more crunch and nutrition.

Weeknight Tomato Sauce

1   medium onion, chopped
½   carrot or 2-3 baby carrots*, diced
2   teaspoons olive oil
¼   teaspoon ground pepper
1   teaspoon sea or kosher salt, divided
1-2   garlic cloves, minced
¼-⅓ cup water or dry white wine

2   28-ounce cans whole, peeled
      tomatoes plus ⅓ can of water
      from each can (this gets
      all of the tomato out)
1-2   tablespoons tomato paste
2   teaspoons sugar
5-8   basil leaves, 1 teaspoon
      basil pesto (see Index), or 1
      tablespoon fresh parsley

*You can add other veggies to this sauce
like peppers, zucchini, mushrooms, etc. to
add extra flavor and a bit more nutrition

Here's a simple tomato sauce that I have been making my whole life. I call it "weeknight" because once you have made it a few times and are familiar with the process, it's easy to make in under an hour. This is how my mom taught me how to make sauce (also known as "gravy"). I hope she doesn't mind my sharing the recipe!

Makes about 3-4 qts.; great for leftovers or freeze for another night. Can be halved.

1. Sauté onions and carrots in olive oil in a large stock or Dutch-oven style pot. Sprinkle pepper over veggies while cooking. Cook until onion is soft, adding a few sprinkles of salt if it's drying out.
2. Add ½ teaspoon of the salt and garlic, stir and cook 1 minute. Add water or wine and cook for 3-5 minutes until liquid evaporates and carrots are softened. If they are not, add more liquid. This softens the carrots and helps to get the flavor from the pan into the sauce.
3. Add the whole, peeled tomatoes and water and cook for 5 minutes on medium. Shut off heat and wait until slightly cooled, about 5-10 minutes.
4. Using an immersion blender, puree tomatoes in the pot, being very careful not to splatter the hot sauce. Start on a low setting and slowly increase the speed. You can also use a regular blender, but you may need to do it in 2 batches.
5. Add tomato paste, sugar, and remaining salt to the pot with the pureed tomatoes. Simmer for 15-30 minutes.
6. At the end, add basil, pesto, or parsley and cook for an additional 5 minutes. Taste and adjust seasoning.

"I've made a similar sauce for all of my pasta sauces in the past, but I like this one far better!" –tester

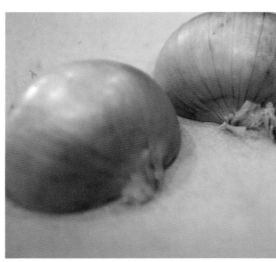

Meat or Bolognese Sauce

1-1½ pounds ground beef or turkey

1   pound pork or chicken Italian sausage (you can use all ground meat if you don't have sausage)

1   medium onion, chopped

½   carrot or 2-3 baby carrots, diced

1   tablespoon olive oil

¼   teaspoon ground black pepper

1   teaspoon sea or kosher salt, divided

1-2   garlic cloves, minced

½   cup dry white wine or water

2   28-ounce cans whole, peeled tomatoes plus ⅓ can of water from each can (this gets all of the tomato out)

1-2   tablespoons tomato paste

2   teaspoons sugar

5-8   basil leaves, 1 teaspoon basil pesto (see opposite page), or 1 tablespoon fresh parsley

If you like a meaty sauce but don't want to spend 3 hours to prepare it, this is a fairly quick sauce that your family will love. It's great with pasta, polenta, or even in your lasagna. It's a variation of the Weeknight Tomato sauce on the prior page.

Makes about 4 quarts; great for leftovers or freeze for another night. Can be halved.

1. Heat a large stock or Dutch-oven style pot to medium-high and add ground meat. Don't move it around in the pan; it will brown better this way. Once it is browned, turn over and cook the other side. After 2 or 3 minutes, start to break up the meat with the side of a spoon. Once cooked, drain the fat, if necessary, and place meat in a medium bowl.

2. Remove pork from casing and cook in the same pot until browned, using the side of a spoon to break into small pieces. Drain fat if necessary. Remove and add to the same bowl as the meat. Keep aside.

3. In the same pot, add olive oil, onion, carrot, and pepper. Stir briefly. Cook until onion is soft, adding a few sprinkles of salt if it's drying out.

4. After about 5-7 minutes, add ½ teaspoon of the salt and garlic, stir, and cook 1 minute. Add wine or water and cook for 3-5 minutes until liquid evaporates and carrots are softened.

5. Add whole, peeled tomatoes and water and cook for 5 minutes over medium heat. Remove from heat and wait until slightly cooled, about 5-10 minutes.

6. Using an immersion blender, puree tomatoes in the pot, being very careful not to splatter the sauce which can be very hot. Start on a low setting and slowly increase the speed. You can also use a regular blender but do it in 2 batches.

7. Add tomato paste, sugar, and salt to the pot with the pureed tomatoes. Add the meat and return to the stove. Simmer for 25-30 minutes.

8. At the end, add basil, pesto, or parsley and cook for an additional 5 minutes. Taste and adjust seasoning.

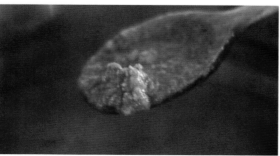

Basil Pesto

2 cups fresh basil leaves
½ cup pine nuts or walnuts, toasted
1 cup grated Parmesan or romano cheese (or a combination of both)
1-2 garlic cloves, chopped in 3-4 pieces
¼ teaspoon sea or kosher salt
¼-½ cup olive oil

Pesto is a great example of how simple ingredients are just simply delicious, and it is so easy to make. You can prepare it in a blender, food processor, or even with an immersion blender. Follow the directions below and use it for pasta, a hearty soup, on bread, with tomatoes, for your tomato sauce, or on a sandwich. It will keep in the fridge about 2 weeks (keep some olive oil on top and it will last even longer), and you can even freeze it.

Makes about 1½ cups

1. Pulse basil in food processor.
2. Add other ingredients and puree. Add more oil until the proper consistency of a paste is formed. Serve.

Variations

SPINACH Instead of all basil, use half spinach and half basil leaves.
SUN-DRIED TOMATO Replace basil with 4 ounces of drained, sun-dried tomatoes packed in oil.
CILANTRO Replace basil with cilantro. Replace pine nuts with cashews. Omit cheese. Add juice from 1 lime.

"So Simple" Tomato Sauce
(THE ITALIAN WAY)

1½ tablespoons good quality extra virgin olive oil
1-2 garlic cloves, minced
1 28-ounce can Italian whole, peeled tomatoes
1 teaspoon sea or kosher salt (or to taste)

I was in Italy and learned this technique. I love the simplicity. If you start this before you boil the water for the pasta, it will be done when the pasta is done cooking. Molto bene! Thank you to Wendy Holloway of The Flavor of Italy for passing it along.

Makes 1 quart

1. Place the garlic and oil in a medium sauce pan. Turn the heat to medium. Cook until it sizzles, only for 30 seconds to a minute.
2. Immediately add the tomatoes and stir. Simmer 5 minutes.
3. Use a fork or potato masher to break up the tomatoes. Simmer on low to medium for about 10 minutes. Stir occasionally.
4. Cover and cook at least another 10 minutes. When you see that some of the oil is separating from the sauce and that it is rising to the top (after about 20 minutes), the sauce is done. Add salt to taste.

Cheese Lasagna

Makes 6-8 servings

RICOTTA FILLING

1	large egg
1½	pounds ricotta
1	cup shredded mozzarella cheese
½	cup grated Parmesan cheese
½	cup milk
1½	teaspoons sea or kosher salt
¾	teaspoon ground black pepper
¾	teaspoon garlic powder

1	quart tomato sauce (jarred, *Weeknight Tomato,* or *Bolognese Sauce*; see Index for recipes)
1¼	cups water
1	teaspoon sea or kosher salt (use less if the sauce is salty)
8-10	ounces no-boil gluten-free lasagna noodles like Tinkyada® or DeBoles®
½-1	cup shredded mozzarella

1. Preheat oven to 350°F.
2. Mix all ingredients of the ricotta filling in a medium bowl.
3. In another medium bowl, mix the sauce with water and salt.
4. Grease a 13" × 9" rectangular baking dish. Ladle 1 cup of sauce on the bottom and spread evenly with a ladle or spoon.
5. Layer with about 3-4 noodles to cover the bottom. Add 1 cup of sauce to cover noodles. Top with half of the ricotta filling and spread evenly.
6. Repeat step 5 using remaining ricotta.
7. Top with noodles and the remaining sauce. Do not add cheese yet.
8. Cut a piece of foil that is big enough to cover the pan. Grease the non-shiny side. Cover the pan with foil, shiny-side up, and bake 45 minutes. Remove foil and top with remaining shredded mozzarella. Bake another 10-15 minutes until cheese is melted and lasagna is bubbling.
9. Let the lasagna rest at least 10 minutes before cutting.

Variations

MEAT

Use the *Bolognese Sauce* (see Index) instead of the tomato sauce. Add 2 cups total of any or all of the following: sliced *Italian Meatballs* (see Index for a recipe), sliced cooked Italian sausage, or crumbled cooked ground meat. Add the meat to the bottom and middle layers of the lasagna.

SPINACH

Add 10 ounces frozen chopped spinach, which has been thawed and squeezed dry, to the ricotta filling.

WHITE

Instead of tomato sauce, use 1 quart of *Cream Sauce* or *Alfredo Sauce* (see Index) mixed with an additional 1¼ cups milk (to help cook the noodles). Add 1-2 cups cooked sautéed veggies to the bottom and middle layers.
Optionally omit ricotta filling.

"Our kids loved it… and it has to be one of the easiest recipes I've ever made. Since I was making it on a weeknight, I went with the jarred sauce— not something I usually do, but it totally worked." –tester

Dairy-Free Lasagna

1   quart tomato sauce (jarred, *Weeknight Tomato,* or *Bolognese Sauce;* see Index for recipes)
1¼   cups water
1   teaspoon sea or kosher salt (use less if the sauce is salty)

8   ounces firm or extra-firm tofu
8-10 ounces no-boil gluten-free lasagna noodles, like Tinkyada® or DeBoles®
1   teaspoon or kosher salt
½   teaspoon ground pepper
½   teaspoon garlic powder
2   cups shredded dairy-free mozzarella cheese, like Daiya®

My daughter has always liked tofu. When she was sensitive to dairy, I replaced the ricotta with tofu. If you can't have soy, try serving with a dairy-free cheese and/or pesto made without dairy.

Makes 6-8 servings

1. Preheat oven to 350°F.
2. In a medium bowl, mix the sauce with water and salt.
3. Cut the tofu into thin slices so that you will have enough to cover the noodles.
4. Grease a 13" × 9" rectangular baking dish. Place 1 cup of sauce on the bottom and spread evenly with a ladle or spoon.
5. Layer with 3-4 noodles to cover the bottom. Add another cup of sauce to cover noodles. Top with half of the tofu. Season the tofu with half of the seasonings (salt, pepper and garlic). Add ½ cup cheese. Top with a little sauce.
6. Repeat step 5.
7. Top with noodles and the remaining sauce. Do not add remaining cheese yet.
8. Cut a piece of foil that is big enough to cover the pan. Grease the non-shiny side. Cover the pan with foil, shiny-side up, and bake 45 minutes. Remove foil and top with remaining shredded mozzarella. Bake another 10-15 minutes until cheese is melted and lasagna is bubbling.
9. Let the lasagna rest at least 10 minutes before cutting.

Chef Tips

Store the ends of loaves of bread in a bag and place in the freezer. When you need breadcrumbs, toast the pieces in the toaster and then chop up; no need to defrost.

You can substitute ground turkey, chicken, or pork for the beef in any of these recipes.

Meatballs and Meatloaf

BINDERS FOR MEATBALLS AND MEATLOAF

Today, you have many options. Before there were gluten-free breadcrumbs, I used gluten-free instant oats or I would make my own crumbs. Some people with celiac disease can't tolerate any oats; in that situation, use the gluten-free breadcrumbs.

If you don't have instant gluten-free oats, it is best to make regular gluten-free oats smaller. Grind in a processor or blender.

If you don't have breadcrumbs, toast 3-4 slices of gluten-free bread and cool slightly. Either chop finely with a knife or grind up in a food processor.

Now that you are an expert at cooking pasta, here are my favorite recipes for meatballs and meatloaf.

Italian Meatballs

This is by far my son's favorite dish. I always joke that I will still be making them for him when he's an adult! If you make them tiny, you can add them to the Chicken Noodle Soup recipe (see Index) without the noodles along with chopped spinach and Parmesan cheese to make Italian Wedding soup.

Makes 12-14 medium or 20-25 small meatballs

2	large eggs
¼-⅓	cup grated Parmesan cheese
¼	cup chopped Italian parsley or 2 tablespoons dry
1	teaspoon minced garlic or ½ teaspoon garlic powder
1	teaspoon sea or kosher salt
½	teaspoon ground pepper
1	pound ground chuck (beef)
¼	pound each ground pork and veal (or ½ pound of one or ½ pound additional beef)
1	cup gluten-free breadcrumbs or gluten-free instant oats
¾	cup milk or milk substitute, plain and unsweetened

1. Preheat the oven to 375°F.
2. Mix eggs, cheese, and seasonings with a fork or whisk. Add remaining ingredients, except milk, and mix. Add ½ cup milk and mix with your hands until well incorporated. If the mixture seems dry, add more milk, up to ¾ cup in total. It's fine if it is a little sticky.
3. Roll meatballs that are about 1½ inches in diameter, about the size of a golf ball.
4. Place on a greased baking sheet or one lined with a silicone mat or parchment paper.
5. Bake for 20 minutes and then turn meatballs over. Bake an additional 10 minutes or until golden brown and internal temperature reaches 165° F.
6. After meatballs are cooked, simmer in *Weeknight Tomato, So Simple Tomato,* or *Bolognese Sauce* (see Index).

Meatballs

2   **large eggs**
1   **teaspoon sea or kosher salt**
½   **teaspoon ground pepper**
¼   **teaspoon garlic powder**
Scant ⅛ teaspoon ground nutmeg
1   **pound ground beef or turkey**
1   **cup gluten-free breadcrumbs**
       or gluten-free instant oats
½-¾ cup milk or milk substitute,
       plain and unsweetened

These meatballs are delicious on their own. I serve them to my kids on a fork and call them "meatball lollipops", something my mom made for me. You can use this recipe for Meatballs Stroganoff (see Index) or simmer in barbecue sauce (see right) to serve as an appetizer or entree.

Makes 12-14 medium or 20-25 small meatballs

1. Preheat the oven to 375°F.
2. Mix eggs and seasonings with a fork or whisk. Add remaining ingredients except milk and mix. Add ¼ cup milk and mix with your hands until well incorporated. If the mixture seems dry, add more milk, up to ¾ cup in total.
3. Roll meatballs that are about 1½ inches in diameter, about the size of a golf ball.
4. Place on a greased baking sheet or one lined with a silicone mat or parchment paper. To help make the meatballs firm, place in the fridge for 30 minutes.
5. Bake for 20 minutes and then turn meatballs over. Bake an additional 10 minutes or until golden brown and the meatballs reach an internal temperature of 165° F.
6. Once cool, serve as is or stick a fork in the middle and eat like a lollipop.

Flavor Variations

ASIAN MEATBALLS

Preheat the oven to 375°F.

Combine the following in a medium bowl:

1 pound ground chicken or light turkey meat, 1 egg white, 1 tablespoon gluten-free soy sauce, 2 teaspoons sesame oil, 1 teaspoon sherry, ¼ teaspoon sea or kosher salt, 2 minced garlic cloves, 2 teaspoons fresh minced ginger, and 2-3 scallions minced (white and some green). Optionally add ¼ cup of minced water chestnuts.

Mix until well combined then mix briskly for 30-60 seconds to help the meatballs to stick together. Follow instructions from step 3 of the Meatball recipe on prior page.

BARBECUE MEATBALLS

Mix the following ingredients in a medium pot. Heat until warm. Add cooked meatballs (see recipe to the left) and simmer for 15-20 minutes.

BARBECUE SAUCE

1 cup ketchup

2 tablespoons brown sugar

2 tablespoons yellow mustard

2 tablespoons molasses or honey

2 teaspoons paprika

2 teaspoons chili powder

1 teaspoon garlic powder

¼ teaspoon ground black pepper

Meatballs Stroganoff

1   recipe *Meatballs* (see prior page), made small
2   cups beef or mushroom broth
½   cup whole milk or milk substitute, plain and unsweetened
¼   teaspoon ground black pepper
¼   teaspoon sea or kosher salt
Pinch of nutmeg

SLURRY
3   tablespoons cornstarch mixed with
3   tablespoons cold water

8   ounces gluten-free pasta

2-3   tablespoons sour cream or dairy-free equivalent

OPTIONAL INGREDIENTS:
1   tablespoon dried chopped parsley for garnish
1   cup peas

Serves 3-4

1. Prepare meatballs. While they bake, proceed with the rest of the recipe.
2. Heat broth, milk, pepper, salt, and nutmeg in a pot on medium low to medium. Heat until broth and milk just start to bubble on the sides (scalding). If you heat the mixture too quickly and boil it, the milk might "break" or look curdled.
3. Meanwhile, make the slurry. Mix water with cornstarch (or any type of starch like potato, tapioca, or arrowroot). Mix until smooth with a small whisk or spoon.
4. Mix slurry right before adding to the heated liquid. Add slurry to the liquid and whisk. Stirring every few minutes, cook 4-6 minutes or until thickened and the starchy texture is no longer present in the sauce. Taste and adjust seasonings.
5. Add meatballs and simmer 10-15 minutes. While the meatballs are simmering, cook the pasta. See *Gluten-Free Pasta Cooking Tips.*
6. Add sour cream at the end and stir. Cook 2 more minutes. Serve over pasta. Optionally garnish with parsley and serve with peas.

Meatloaf

1-1½ pounds ground meat
1-2   large eggs (use 2 eggs if you use 1 ½ pounds of meat or if you use lean meat)
1   cup gluten-free breadcrumbs or gluten-free instant oats
½   cup milk or milk substitute, plain and unsweetened
½   cup ketchup plus 3-4 tablespoons for the top
½   teaspoon sea or kosher salt
¼   teaspoon ground black pepper
1-2   tablespoons yellow mustard
1   tablespoon gluten-free soy sauce

OPTIONAL: 1 package frozen, chopped spinach, thawed and squeezed dry

OPTIONAL: Top with ½-1 cup of any shredded cheese during the last 15 minutes of baking

I love making this with turkey but you can use any ground meat. If you use turkey or chicken breast (white meat), you should use the extra egg since breast meat is so lean. The combination of flavors is really tasty; this is a dish that most children and adults enjoy.

Serves 4-6

1. Preheat oven to 350°F. Grease a 13" × 9" or loaf pan.
2. Mix all ingredients together using only ½ cup of ketchup and ½ cup of breadcrumbs or oats (the binder). Optionally, add the chopped spinach to the mixture. If the mixture is not stiff, add more breadcrumbs or oats. If it's too stiff, add more milk. It should hold its shape together.
3. Form into a 5" × 13" rectangle in the middle of the pan, or place in a loaf pan. Top with additional ketchup.
4. Bake for 35-45 minutes or until meatloaf has started to brown and has reached and internal temperature of at least 165°F.
5. Let meat rest 10 minutes before cutting. Serve with *Mashed Potatoes* and/or *Wild Mushroom Marsala Sauce* (see Index).

Chef Tip

To make sure your meatball or meatloaf is seasoned well, cook a small piece in a fry pan first and taste. Adjust seasoning if needed.

Vegetarian Shepherd's Pie made with mushrooms and walnuts instead of meat

For extra nutrition, substitute an equal amount of chopped cauliflower for some of the potatoes, for example 2 cups. Add to the water with the potatoes and boil together, making sure both are tender before mashing.

Browning Ground Meat

Heat a large pan to medium-high first. If you are using a lean ground meat, add 2 teaspoons of vegetable or olive oil. Add ground meat in small walnut-sized pieces. If you run out of room, do this in batches. Reduce heat if fat from meat is splattering outside of the pan.

Don't move the meat in the pan; just leave it. It will brown better this way.

Once it is browned, turn over and cook the other side. After 2 or 3 minutes, start to break up the meat with the side of a spoon.

Once cooked, proceed with your recipe.

Shepherd's Pie

POTATOES

6-8 (1½ – 2 pounds) russet potatoes, washed, peeled, and cut into pieces
2 teaspoons sea or kosher salt
4 tablespoons unsalted butter or butter substitute
¼-½ cup milk or milk substitute, plain and unsweetened
¼-½ teaspoon sea or kosher salt
¼ teaspoon white or black pepper

MEAT

2 teaspoons olive oil
1 small onion, chopped
¼ teaspoon ground black pepper
¼ teaspoon herbs de Provence or dried thyme
1¼-1½ pounds ground beef or turkey
OPTIONAL: ¼ cup cooking wine like Marsala, sherry, or dry white wine
1½ cups beef or chicken broth

SLURRY

2 tablespoons cornstarch mixed with
2 tablespoons cold water

1 tablespoon unsalted butter or butter substitute

VEGETABLES

2 cups slightly thawed veggies like frozen corn, carrots and peas, and/or chopped spinach (or any combination of this)

Chef Tips

This dish can be made ahead, refrigerated, and then baked. Add 10-15 minutes additional baking time.

Make sure to read the recipe in its entirety; the timing is important so everything is done at the same time.

In England, Shepherd's Pie is actually made with lamb and Cottage Pie with beef. In America, most people call this Shepherd's Pie. I like adding a thickened pan gravy to the meat. This sauce bubbles up and gives a wonderful flavor to the whole dish.

Besides being able to use any ground meat, you can substitute sautéed mushrooms for the meat to make it vegetarian. You can use many different vegetables, not just corn. I use whatever is in the freezer (including corn) like peas, carrots, chopped spinach, or a combination of any of these. The end result is dinner in a single baking dish that puts a smile on everyone's face.

Serves 6-8

1. In a large pot, cover potatoes with water, add salt, and cover. Bring to boil and lower to a simmer. While the potatoes cook, prepare the meat.
2. Heat a large sauté pan to medium and add oil, onion, pepper, and herbs or thyme. Cook until the onion is translucent and brown. Remove and place in a small bowl.
3. In the same pan, brown ground meat (see opposite page for *Browning Ground Meat*). Drain fat if necessary. Add onions and stir. Add the cooking wine, if using, and cook until it is evaporated.
4. Add broth and bring to a simmer. Add the slurry and cook for 2-3 minutes or until thickened. Taste and adjust for seasoning; add more salt and pepper if necessary. Once sauce has thickened, turn off heat.
5. Preheat oven to 350°F. Grease a 13" × 9" baking dish.
6. Make the mashed potatoes. Drain the potatoes and add butter, milk, salt, and pepper and mash. Taste and adjust seasonings.
7. Place ground meat mixture in the baking dish. Add veggies, distributing evenly over the meat. Top with mashed potatoes and spread evenly. Optionally, run a fork the length of the potatoes to make a pattern.
8. Bake in oven until bubbly and the top starts to brown, about 25-30 minutes. You can also broil the top to brown potatoes. Allow to rest for at least 10 minutes before serving.

"I've never been a big fan of Shepherd's Pie, but one bite of Amy's dish changed my mind. The addition of herbs de Provence in the meat and cauliflower in the potatoes added even more delicious flavor. My family loved it!" –tester

Chili

2	teaspoons olive or vegetable oil
1	medium onion, chopped
1	carrot, diced
1	red or green pepper, chopped
¼-½	teaspoon each: ground pepper, oregano, and coriander
1	teaspoon cumin
2	tablespoons mild chili powder
1-1½	teaspoons sea or kosher salt
1-2	garlic cloves, minced
1	pound lean ground beef or turkey
1	15-ounce can diced tomatoes
1	15-ounce can tomato sauce
2	15-ounce cans beans, drained and rinsed (kidney, black, and/or pinto)
3	cups broth or water
1-2	tablespoons tomato paste

OPTIONAL INGREDIENTS: If you like a spicier chili, add ¼ teaspoon spicy chili powder or cayenne pepper with the other herbs and spices in step 1.

Makes about 2 quarts

1. Heat a large soup or stock pot to medium. Add oil and then onion, carrot, and pepper and give it a quick stir or shake. Sprinkle with herbs and spices (but not the garlic or salt) and stir. Cook until vegetables are soft. Add garlic and salt; cook for 1 minute. Remove from pot and place in a medium bowl.

2. Make sure the pan is hot again and add ground meat, being careful not to overcrowd the pan (see Index for *Browning Ground Meat*). Cook meat until brown then crumble with the back of a spoon.

3. Once the meat is cooked through, add the reserved veggies, diced tomatoes, tomato sauce, beans, broth or water, and tomato paste. Bring to a boil, lower to a simmer, and cook covered, 20-30 minutes.

4. Taste chili and adjust the seasonings, including salt. If the chili looks dry, add more broth or water.

Cornbread

1	cup cornmeal
¾	cup *Amy's Gluten-Free Flour Blend*
2	tablespoons-¼ cup sugar (use less if you do not like sweet cornbread)
2	teaspoons baking powder
½	teaspoon xanthan gum
½	teaspoon salt
1	egg, lightly beaten
1	cup milk or milk substitute, plain and unsweetened
¼	cup vegetable oil or melted butter

OPTIONAL INGREDIENTS:

½	cup frozen corn, slightly thawed or fresh corn, cut from the cob
½	cup shredded cheddar
¼	cup diced mild green chiles

Makes one 8" × 8" pan

1. Preheat the oven to 400°F. Grease a 9" × 9" or 8" × 8" square pan.

2. In a medium bowl, combine the dry ingredients (first 6 ingredients). In another small to medium bowl, combine the egg, milk, and oil and whisk to combine.

3. Pour the wet ingredients into the dry ingredients and stir. Add the optional ingredients if you are using. Stir briskly for about 20-30 seconds. Pour the batter into the prepared pan.

4. Bake for 14-16 minutes until the cornbread begins to pull away from the sides of the pan, is golden in color, and springs back to the touch. If you overcook, it will be dry.

5. Cool in pan 10 minutes before cutting.

Note:

To make into muffins, prepare a 12-cup muffin tin by either greasing or placing liners inside. Fill cups with batter about ⅔ full. Bake for 14-16 minutes or until muffin springs back.

1 recipe of *Chili* (make first)
1 recipe of *Cornbread* (do not mix
batter until chili is done)

Chef Tips

After making this a few times, here's
what I have learned. The cornbread
will absorb a lot of liquid, thus making it very moist. But, it can make the
chili dry, leaving only beans and meat.
Make sure the chili is not too thick;
you can always add more broth or
water. The other option is to make
the chili pie and then serve it with the
reserved chili. If you like chili and cornbread, I have a feeling you will like this.

In my recipes, when you see a range
of herbs or spices, use more or less,
depending upon your taste; you can
always add more at the end.

Chili Pie

*My testers loved this recipe. I created this dish when my children were
very young. On one occasion, I made it for a playgroup dinner which
consisted of mostly 2- and 4-year-olds along with their mothers. It was
amazing to see how much everyone enjoyed a flavorful chili made
with plenty of vegetables and a gluten-free cornbread. It was truly a
"family chef" moment.*

Makes 6-8 servings

1. Pour about half (1 quart) of the chili into a greased 11" × 7" pan
(you may not be able to spread the cornbread evenly over a 13" × 9"
pan). Keep reserved chili warm. Set aside for at least 15 minutes. Do
not make the cornbread until the chili has cooled slightly. If you
place the cornbread batter on hot chili, it will sink. If you mix the batter ahead, it will get too thick and the leavening will start reacting.
2. Preheat oven to 400°F.
3. Mix cornbread according to recipe. Pour batter over chili and
spread evenly. Bake for 16-18 minutes or until cornbread is light
brown on top and it springs back when touched. The chili should be
bubbling.
4. Remove from oven and cool for 10 minutes before serving.
5. Pour 4-8 ounces of chili into individual bowls. Portion chili pie on
top and serve.

Burrito Casserole

1   cup uncooked brown or
white rice, or quinoa
1   pound ground beef or turkey
1   tablespoon mild chili powder
1   teaspoon paprika
½   teaspoon each garlic powder, cumin,
coriander, and black pepper
1   teaspoon sea or kosher salt
1   small can of mild green
chiles, chopped
½   cup sour cream (omit for dairy-free
or use a plain yogurt substitute)
½   cup *Ranch Dressing* (see
Index for recipe)
1   15-ounce can beans like black, pinto,
or kidney, drained and rinsed
½   cup salsa
½   cup shredded cheddar or Monterey
Jack cheese, or cheese substitute

Chef Tips

If you are short on time, this dish can be microwaved for 5-6 minutes.

For extra protein, use 2 cans of beans.

You can also use *Mexican Brown Rice* (see Index) for the base.

One thing that can be missed on a gluten-free diet is a burrito. One idea I had is to leave the tortilla out of the picture entirely and just focus on the filling. This "deconstructed" burrito casserole is healthy, family-friendly, and versatile. Once the rice and meat are cooked, it only takes minutes to assemble and about 20 minutes to heat. Dinner is served!

Serves 4-6

1. Cook rice or quinoa (see Index for *Cooking Grains*). Prep other ingredients while it cooks.
2. About 10 minutes before rice or quinoa is done, heat large sauté pan on medium to medium high heat. Place pieces of the ground meat in the pan (see Index for *Browning Ground Meat*). Sprinkle all of the spices except the salt over the meat. Do not stir (this gives it great browning and flavor).
3. When both sides of the meat have browned, use the side of a spoon to break the meat up into smaller pieces. Drain fat if necessary. Add salt and ½ cup of water. Cook for 3-4 minutes and shut heat off.
4. Preheat oven to 350°F and grease a large casserole dish.
5. Place rice or quinoa in bottom of casserole dish. Top with meat and green chiles, pressing down. Mix sour cream and ranch dressing (if using) and spread on top of meat. Add beans and salsa and top with cheese.
6. Cover and bake 20-30 minutes or until cheese is melted and casserole is bubbling. Remove cover and cook 5 more minutes. Allow to rest for 5 minutes before serving.

Flour Tortillas/ Flatbread

1½ cups **Amy's Gluten-Free Flour Blend**
½ cup cornstarch plus a little
  more for dusting
2 teaspoons xanthan gum
1 teaspoon sugar
1 teaspoon salt

¾-1 cup warm water
Oil or shortening for cooking tortillas

"All I can say is yum! The first bite brought me back to my Mom's German dish she makes called Spaetzle. My daughter and her friend couldn't wait to try them; they loved it. Then my husband came home and I had to take them away from him and hide the rest." –tester

This recipe adapted from one by Mary Frances of Gluten-Free Cooking School.

Makes 8 tortillas. This recipe doubles well

1. Place the dry ingredients (first 5 ingredients) in a large mixing bowl and whisk together.
2. Slowly add ¾ cup of warm water to the bowl and mix together with one hand. Continue mixing until a ball forms. If it's too dry, add more water, a little at a time. If it's very sticky, add more cornstarch. Keep covered if you are not going to cook the tortillas right away.
3. Heat cast iron pan, flat pan, or grill over medium to medium-high heat.
4. Working with 1-2 pieces of dough at a time, roll pieces of dough, about 1½-2 inches in diameter, into balls.
5. Place a large piece of wax paper that can be folded over onto itself in a tortilla press. Sprinkle with corn starch on both sides. Put dough ball in the middle and press down a little to flatten. Fold wax paper on top and then use tortilla press to flatten. If you don't have a tortilla press, roll the dough to 1/8", i.e. very thin, between two pieces of plastic wrap. Press or roll only 1 or 2 at a time as the tortilla might stick. It's best to roll them and cook immediately.
6. Put a little shortening or oil in the hot pan. As soon as it melts, place tortilla onto the pan. Cook each side about 2-3 minutes or until it has started puffing up and the bottom side is developing brown spots. Flip the tortilla and cook the other side until it is toasty as well. When tortilla is done, place on a plate while you make the others.
7. Repeat with remaining dough, adding more oil to the pan as needed.

Beef Stew

2 tablespoons white rice flour
2 tablespoons potato starch
½-1 teaspoon sea or kosher salt
½ teaspoon ground pepper
½-1 teaspoon herbs de Provence
or a combination of dried
thyme and oregano

1 pound beef stew meat, patted dry
1 tablespoon olive or vegetable oil
2 tablespoons dry sherry
or wine (optional)
2 cups beef broth
1 15-ounce can diced
tomatoes with juice
½ medium onion, chopped
3 carrots, cut into circles, ¼" thick
1 pound Yukon Gold or red
potatoes, about 3 or 4, cubed
1 cup each fresh or frozen corn
and peas, thawed slightly

This delicious stew can be made in a slow cooker or on the stove top; it will certainly give you a "warm kitchen" feeling. I always prefer the slow cooker but know that not everyone has one. If you make it on the stove top, make sure to stir it every 30 minutes or so. Take the time to sear the meat first; besides giving the dish color, it also gives it great flavor. Coating the meat in the flour and starch mixture helps to thicken the stew in the end.

Serves 3-4

SLOW COOKER VERSION

1. Mix flour, starch, salt, pepper, and herbs in a bowl with a lid or sealable plastic bag. Place beef inside, close lid or seal, and shake to coat.
2. Heat oil in a large sauté pan to medium high heat. Place beef in pan, reserving the flour mixture. Cook meat 2-3 minutes on each side or until just browned. Optionally, add sherry or wine and cook for 1 more minute.
3. Place broth, tomatoes, onion, and carrots in a crock pot. Sprinkle 1 tablespoon of the reserved flour mixture (discard the remainder) on top and stir. Add beef. Cover and cook 3 hours on high or 4-5 hours on low.
4. During the last hour of cooking, add potatoes and cook 30 additional minutes or until tender. Add corn and peas and cook 10-15 minutes or until heated.
5. Taste and adjust seasonings; it might need more salt at the end.

STOVE-TOP VERSION

1. Mix flour, starch, salt, pepper, and herbs in a bowl with a lid or sealable plastic bag. Place beef inside, close lid or seal, and shake to coat.
2. Heat oil in a dutch oven or large stock pot over medium high heat. Place beef in pan, reserving the flour mixture. Cook meat 2-3 minutes on each side or until just browned. Optionally add sherry or wine and cook for 1 more minute.
3. Lower heat slightly and add broth, tomatoes, onion, and carrots to the pot. Add 1 tablespoon of reserved flour mixture (discard the remainder) and stir. Bring to a boil, lower to a simmer, and cover. Cook 2 hours, stirring every 30 minutes or until meat is almost tender.
4. Add potatoes, bring back to a simmer, and cook uncovered for 20 minutes or until the potatoes are just tender. If the stew is very thick, keep covered and/or add another cup of broth. Add corn and peas and cook 10 minutes or until heated.
5. Taste and adjust seasonings; it might need more salt at the end.

Cooking Poultry

Sometimes with gluten-free it's just safer to eat at home than in a restaurant. Knowing how to cook the basics is important.

This part of the chapter starts with a Cooking Lesson which might just change the way you cook at home. See the following pages for more information on how this one technique can create many dishes. There are other recipes as well which are just simply delicious.

Cooking Lesson

HOW TO SAUTÉ

To me, this is where the magic happens. Follow the steps on this page to learn how to make extremely tasty chicken. Use the Flavor Profile Variations for Seasonings *(see Index) and follow the same technique but with different ingredients to create new dishes.*

The method on the page opposite is best suited for chicken breast because of this cut's lean properties. Chicken is versatile and can be very flavorful. However, if cooked improperly, it can be literally hard to chew.

Chicken breast is leaner than thigh meat and works better for a quick sauté or light braise. Here's what you need to know about sautéing meat:

- Pieces should be uniform in thickness; if pieces are thick, place the meat between sheets of wax paper, plastic wrap, or in a freezer bag and pound with a mallet or a heavy bottomed pan to flatten.

- Cook in a large pan or cook in batches; if the pan is crowded, the meat will steam not sauté.

- Use some fat but not too much. 2 teaspoons to 1 tablespoon of oil should be plenty.

- If cooking in batches, leave the cooked meat on a plate, loosely covered with foil.

How To Make It...
Easy as 1, 2, 3

SAUTÉ MEAT

1 Season the meat. Use the *Flavor Profile Variations for Seasonings* (see Index) for ideas.

2 Cook in a hot pan and step away from the stove!

3 Turn over and finish cooking.

Chef Tips

ONE CLEAN AND ONE DIRTY HAND

When cutting chicken (or other raw meat), try to use one hand to handle the chicken and use one hand for the knife (for example, hold the chicken with your left hand while you cut with your right hand). That way, one hand stays clean while the other is dirty. Use the clean hand to touch utensils, stove knobs and the spices. Use the dirty hand to move the chicken.

Do not touch anything with your dirty hand besides the chicken to avoid cross contamination. Make sure to wash your hands and anything that has touched the raw chicken with hot, soapy water.

Sautéed Italian Chicken

½ teaspoon each oregano, thyme, ground pepper, and garlic powder (or about 2 teaspoons Italian seasoning blend)
½ teaspoon sea or kosher salt
1 pound boneless, skinless chicken breasts or tenders, trimmed of fat and/or connective tissue, flattened with a meat mallet
2 teaspoons olive or vegetable oil

OPTIONAL SAUCE INGREDIENTS:
¼ cup white wine or juice from ½ fresh lemon for deglazing, 1-2 tablespoons unsalted butter, and/ or 1-2 tablespoons drained capers

Other Proteins for Sautéing

For these recipes, you can use other lean proteins such as the following:

- **Peeled and deveined shrimp**
- **Turkey tenders cut into strips**
- **Lean steak like filet or sirloin**
- **Pork cutlet**
- **Extra firm tofu, pressed, to remove excess water**

Serves 3-4

1. Mix herbs, spices and salt in a small bowl. Sprinkle half over chicken (see chef tip on prior page for how to handle raw chicken).
2. Heat medium sauté pan to medium or medium high. Once the pan is hot, add the oil and quickly place the chicken in the pan, seasoning side down, being careful not to crowd the pan. Cook in batches if necessary. If using a non-stick pan, add oil and then heat pan. As soon as oil is hot, add chicken.
3. Do not move chicken in the pan. Sprinkle remaining seasoning on other side of chicken. You can save any extra seasoning as long as it has not touched the raw chicken. Adjust heat if necessary so that you can hear the chicken cooking but so that it's not burning.
4. Once chicken is fragrant and beginning to turn white on the edges, turn over and cook the other side. The cooked side should be brown. Again, do not move around in the pan and try not to overcook.
5. Cooked chicken will be firm when you press it. If it's not done, it will feel soft. Try to resist the temptation to cut into it; you'll lose a lot of the natural juices.
6. Once the chicken is cooked, you can deglaze the pan by adding ¼ cup white wine or the juice from ½ fresh lemon. Let that cook for 1 minute, remove from heat, then add 1-2 tablespoons unsalted butter and capers. This creates a quick and delicious sauce.

✓ *Recommended Side Dishes for Chicken (see Index for recipes)*

ITALIAN

Pesto with pasta

Polenta

Cauliflower mashed potatoes

MEXICAN

Mexican brown rice

Flour tortillas

Millet mixed with Cilantro pesto

GREEK

Sun-dried tomato pesto and pasta

Chard and quinoa salad

Lentil and rice pilaf

INDIAN

Sweet potato millet cakes

Almond quinoa pilaf

Flour tortillas

Sautéed Chicken

WITH APRICOT DIJON GLAZE

1   recipe of *Sautéed Italian Chicken* (see prior page)

½   cup reduced-sugar apricot preserves or jelly
2   tablespoons Dijon mustard
1   tablespoon red wine vinegar
Sea or kosher salt and ground black pepper to taste

Serves 3-4

This recipe works well with a thicker piece of chicken, for example, a breast that has not been pounded. When the sauce is added and the chicken is covered, it enables the chicken to finish cooking by braising. The process will keep the chicken juicy and moist.

While the chicken is cooking, mix the preserves, mustard, vinegar, salt, and pepper. Once the chicken is almost all of the way cooked, pour the sauce over the chicken. Cover and lower the heat. Simmer at least 5 minutes and/or until the chicken is fully cooked, up to 20 minutes.

Chicken is done when it feels firm when pressed and/or reaches an internal temperature of at least 165°F.

Flavor Profile Variations for Seasonings

Follow the steps for the *Sautéed Italian Chicken* on the prior page but use the seasonings below to get the following flavors.

MEXICAN/FAJITA

FOR THE SEASONING, use ½ teaspoon each : cumin, coriander, oregano, garlic, salt, and pepper.

Squeeze lime on top to finish. Optionally add salsa and/or guacamole.

GREEK

FOR THE SEASONING, use ½ teaspoon each: oregano, dill, thyme, and salt.

Squeeze fresh lemon on top to finish and add crumbled feta cheese, chopped tomatoes, and/or kalamata olives.

INDIAN

FOR THE SEASONING, use ¼ teaspoon each: coriander, curry powder or turmeric, and ground ginger combined with ½ tsp. each: cumin, salt, and pepper.

Top with plain yogurt.

Chicken Parmesan

For one pound of boneless, skinless chicken breast patted dry:
(see Index for Other Proteins for Sautéing)

FLOURED CHICKEN

In a shallow bowl, mix 1-2 tablespoons each potato starch and white rice flour (use more if the chicken pieces are small), ½ teaspoon salt, and 1/8 teaspoon ground pepper. Dredge dry chicken in flour mixture, brushing off extra. Sauté chicken in 2-3 teaspoons of olive or vegetable oil until golden on each side; add more oil if necessary.

- Try adding ½ cup of chicken broth or ¼ cup of dry white wine at the end to make a super juicy dish. Cook until liquid reduces, about 2-3 minutes.

- Add broth or wine to the chicken as directed above. Serve with the *Lemon Caper Sauce* (see Index) for a chicken piccata style dish.

BATTERED CHICKEN

Mix 1/3 cup cornstarch or potato starch, ½ teaspoon sea or kosher salt, ¼ teaspoon ground pepper, and 2 large egg whites. Dip chicken in batter and then immediately into a pan of hot oil. Cook on each side until batter is golden.

- Serve with the *Teriyaki Marinade and Sauce* or *Spicy Orange Sauce* (see Index for recipes).

BREADED CHICKEN

Place in each of 3 separate shallow bowls: floured chicken mixture above, 1 beaten egg and 1 cup of gluten-free breadcrumbs or crushed gluten-free corn flakes. Use the recipe for *Chicken Tenders* (see following page) for cooking instructions.

- Use to make Chicken Parmesan: top each piece with 2-3 tablespoons of tomato sauce and shredded mozzarella cheese. Bake in a 375°F oven until cheese is melted and sauce is bubbling.

- Top with a piece of sliced ham, steamed broccoli or asparagus, and *Cream Sauce* (see Index).

- Place a slice of ham and Swiss cheese in the center of a piece of raw chicken which has been pounded flat. Roll up, secure with toothpicks, and bread using above directions. Bake at 375°F for 20-30 minutes or until internal temperature is 165°F. Serve with *Creamy Mustard Sauce* (See Index) See photo #4 on the opposite page.).

What is…

1 SAUTÉED: Can be prepared plain or seasoned and cooked in a pan with a small amount of oil.

2 FLOURED: Dredged in flour seasoned with at least salt and pepper; creates a crust. Use white rice flour and potato starch or plain white rice flour.

3 BATTERED: Dipped in a batter and then placed into a hot pan with a layer of oil.

4 BREADED: Floured protein is dipped in beaten egg and then bread crumbs. Can be sautéed, fried, or baked.

Chicken Tenders

(SAUTÉED OR BAKED)

Serves 3-4

1	**pound boneless skinless chicken breast or tenders**
2	**tablespoons white rice flour**
2	**tablespoons potato starch**
½	**teaspoon sea or kosher salt**
¼	**teaspoon ground black pepper**
1	**large egg**
1	**tablespoon milk or milk substitute, plain and unsweetened**
2	**cups gluten-free corn flakes, crushed or ground up**
1-2	**tablespoons olive or vegetable oil for sautéing**

1. Slice chicken breasts into strips; if using tenders, proceed to the next step. Pat dry if wet.

2. Mix flour, starch, salt, and pepper in a shallow bowl. Place egg and milk in another shallow bowl and beat lightly. Place corn flake crumbs in another shallow bowl.

3. Bread the chicken. Take 3-4 pieces of chicken and first dip in flour mixture. Shake excess. Dip in egg and then corn flake crumbs. Place breaded chicken on plate or tray until all chicken is coated.

4. TO SAUTÉ: Place 1 tablespoon of oil in a large sauté pan. Heat to medium heat. Add one piece of chicken to the oil. If chicken does not make a sizzle sound, let the pan heat up more.
Add chicken pieces but don't crowd pan. Don't move chicken; allow to brown. Turn once and cook until heated through. Place on a piece of paper towel on a plate and place chicken on this plate to absorb some of the oil. Use more oil if needed.

TO BAKE: Preheat oven to 425°F and prepare a baking sheet with parchment paper or a silicone baking sheet. Once tenders are breaded in step 3, place on baking sheet. For crispier tenders, drizzle with 2-3 teaspoons of olive or vegetable oil. Bake for 15-18 minutes or until golden brown and crisp, turning once.

5. To keep tenders warm or to crisp up, place tenders on a baking sheet and place in a 350°F oven for 5-10 minutes.

6. Serve with *So Simple Tomato Sauce*, *Spicy Orange Sauce*, or *Barbecue Sauce* (see Index).

Sauteing the tenders will make them more crisp. Testers liked this method better. You can keep them warm in the oven after they are cooked or if they get soggy.

Chicken Pot Pie

(BISCUIT TOPPING)

CHICKEN POT PIE FILLING
3   cups chicken broth
2   cups milk or milk substitute,
     plain and unsweetened

SLURRY:
**Mix ¼ cup cornstarch with
¼ cup cold water**

½   teaspoon each dried thyme and sage
     or 1 teaspoon poultry seasoning
¼   teaspoon black pepper
1   teaspoon sea or kosher salt
2-3 cups cooked chicken,
     chopped or shredded
2   cups mixed frozen vegetables
     like a combination of peas, corn,
     and carrots, thawed slightly

***Note: The biscuits will absorb the
stew. If using *Hearty Chicken Stew*
(see Index) , add at least 1 cup more
broth and/or milk or the stew will be
too dry. For every cup of additional
liquid, add 1 tablespoon each of
cornstarch and water to step 5.**

DROP BISCUIT TOPPING
⅓   cup unsalted butter (or
     shortening for dairy-free)

DRY INGREDIENTS
1½ cups white rice flour
½   cup potato starch
1   tablespoon white sugar
2   teaspoons baking powder
1   teaspoon sea or kosher salt
1   teaspoon xanthan gum

WET INGREDIENTS
⅔   cup whole milk or milk substitute,
     plain and unsweetened
3   large eggs
1   teaspoon white vinegar

CHICKEN POT PIE FILLING

You can also use Hearty Chicken Stew (see Index) for the filling.

Serves 6-8

1. Place chicken broth, milk, and seasonings in a medium to large soup pot over medium heat. Slowly heat broth and milk, being careful not to heat too quickly; otherwise the milk might "break" or curdle.
2. Meanwhile, make the slurry in a small bowl or cup. When you see little bubbles on the edges of the broth-milk mixture, stir slurry first, and then slowly whisk it into the pot. Simmer and continue cooking, stirring occasionally. See *How to Make a Slurry* (see Index) to learn more about thickening sauces.
3. Add chicken and vegetables. Simmer about 5 minutes or until all ingredients are hot. Taste and season with additional salt, pepper, sage, and thyme. Simmer 20 minutes.
4. Preheat oven to 375°F.
5. Place cooked stew into a greased baking dish that's deep enough to hold 2 quarts, for example a 13" × 9" pan.
6. Prepare Drop Biscuit Topping. When dough is ready, proceed to next step.
7. Portion biscuit batter with a spoon or scooper by dropping on top of stew; you should be able to portion about 16 biscuits on top.
8. Bake for 14-16 minutes or until biscuits are golden and puffy.

DROP BISCUIT TOPPING

1. Place butter or shortening in the freezer for 5 minutes to chill while you measure the other ingredients.
2. Place dry ingredients in the bowl of a food processor and pulse to mix. If you don't have a processor, place the dry ingredients in a medium bowl and mix with a whisk to combine.
3. In another small bowl, mix the eggs, milk, and vinegar to combine.
4. Add cold butter or shortening to the processor. Pulse for 10-20 seconds or until butter or shortening is chopped. The mixture should look like grated Parmesan cheese. If you don't have a food processor, use a pastry blender to blend the butter and shortening with the flour mixture, or use two knifes to "cut" the shortening and butter into the flour mixture.
5. Remove butter and flour mixture and add to a medium sized bowl. Add wet ingredients and mix until a dough forms. Follow directions above from step 7.

Chicken Pot Pie

(PASTRY TOPPING)

If you have missed chicken pot pie, look no further. It requires some planning since the pie crust has to be chilled but the end result is something you might find in a restaurant. If given the choice, my daughter might eat this every night! Of course, you can always use a pre-made gluten-free pie crust.

You can make the pot pies in a variety of ways: the stew topped with the pie crust, the stew inside of a pie (bottom and top crusts) or individual pies in ramekins with the pie crust on top. If you make the pot pie in a deep pie dish, you can freeze any extra pie crust for another use . Regardless of the style, hopefully you and your family will be as enthusiastic as ours.

Serves 4-6

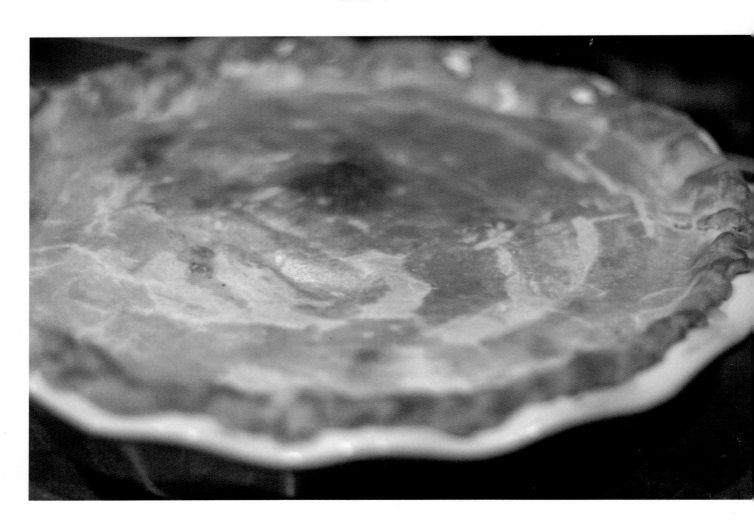

1¾ cups **Amy's Gluten-Free Flour Blend**
¾ teaspoon **xanthan gum**
½ teaspoon **sea or kosher salt**
4 tablespoons **unsalted butter, cut into pieces**
4 tablespoons **vegetable shortening (or use 8 tablespoons total of butter or shortening)**
1 large **egg, lightly beaten**
2 teaspoons **white or apple cider vinegar**
1-2 tablespoons **ice water**

1 recipe of **Chicken Pot Pie Filling (see prior page)**

Egg wash: 1 egg beaten with 1 tablespoon milk or water

PIE CRUST

1. Start by making the crust first. Place butter and shortening in a small bowl. Place in the freezer to get extra cold for 5 minutes. By the time you are done measuring the flours, it will be cold enough.

2. Add flours, xanthan gum, and salt to a food processor. Pulse a few times to mix. Alternatively, mix this in a medium bowl.

3. Add very cold shortening and butter to the processor. Pulse for 10-20 seconds or until shortening and butter is chopped. The mixture should look like grated Parmesan cheese. If you don't have a food processor, use a pastry blender to blend the butter and shortening with the flour mixture, or use two knifes to "cut" the shortening and butter into the flour mixture.

4. Remove butter and flour mixture and add to a medium sized bowl.

5. Mix the egg and vinegar in a small bowl. Add 1 tablespoon of the ice water, reserving the last tablespoon if needed. Add this to the butter and flour mixture, using your hands to mix. Dough should stick together well. If it doesn't, add a few drops of water until it does. Note: See *Chef Tips: Pie Crust* page 244, for tips.

6. Divide dough in half and shape each piece into a disc; if you are using a deep pie dish, roll only one disc. Wrap each disc in plastic wrap and place in fridge for at least 30 minutes or up to 2 days.

7. Make the *Chicken Pot Pie Filling* (see prior page) and cool slightly.

8. Take the crusts out 5 minutes before you are ready to roll. You may not use all of it.

9. Preheat oven to 375°F. Decide if you want to use a deep dish pie with a top and bottom, a deep dish pie with just a top, two regular pie dishes with tops, or four individual pot pies.

10. Place cooked stew in pie dish(es) or ramekins.

11. Roll out dough to 1/8" thickness between two pieces of plastic. Make sure to roll out dough ½" bigger than the ramekin or pie dish. If using the ramekins, cut circles that are ½" bigger than the ramekin so that you can fold the dough over the top.

12. Carefully place dough on top and crimp the dough on the side, pressing it to make it stick. Brush the dough with the egg wash and make 3-4 slits in the top.

13. Place the pie dishes or ramekins on a baking sheet and bake for 20-25 minutes, or until crust is cooked and light brown, and the filling is bubbling hot.

14. Let rest for 5-10 minutes before eating.

"The fish turned out great. My husband really liked the coating. It browned nicely and was very easy to whip together." –tester

Fish, Chips and Mushy Peas

1   **pound firm white fish like cod, haddock, or flounder, cut into 2 or 3 pieces**

BATTER
2   **teaspoons corn starch**
1   **large egg white**
½   **teaspoon sea or kosher salt**
1-2   **tablespoons vegetable oil for frying (something appropriate for high heat like safflower, peanut, or vegetable shortening)**

My (English) husband and I really miss fish and chips. I borrowed the batter part from another recipe and decided to try it with the fish. The result was delicious. My daughter's quote was, "This is better than ketchup!" If you are in England, fish and chips are also served with a side of mushy peas. Give it a try for a bit of a traditional English meal. I personally love fried fish with Coleslaw (see Index for my recipe).

Serves 3-4

1. Place a paper towel on a large plate. Place fish on top and pat dry.
2. Mix egg white, cornstarch, and salt in a bowl large enough for the fish pieces.
3. Heat a medium to large pan with the oil on medium high heat. When the oil is hot but not smoking, coat the fish in the batter and cook on each side until each piece is golden brown, about 2-3 minutes per side, depending upon the thickness of the fish. You may need to do this in two batches.
4. Fish is done when the outside is golden and the fish is firm. Place cooked fish on another plate lined with either a paper towel or brown paper bag.

2-3   **russet potatoes, peeled, cut into strips, rinsed and dried**
1   **tablespoon oil**
½   **teaspoon sea or kosher salt**
¼   **teaspoon ground black pepper**

"CHIPS" (BAKED FRENCH FRIES)

Preheat oven to 450°F. Toss potatoes with oil, salt, and pepper. Place on a baking sheet lined with parchment or a silicone baking mat in a single layer. Bake 15 minutes, stir, then bake another 15-20 minutes or until brown and crisp.

2   **cups peas (fresh or frozen)**
¼   **cup milk or milk substitute, plain and unsweetened**
1   **tablespoon butter or butter substitute**
Salt and pepper to taste

MUSHY PEAS

Simmer peas gently for about 3 minutes. If using fresh, cook longer, until they are bright green and tender.
Drain and add to food processor or blender along with remaining ingredients. Pulse until creamy and thick and there are small pieces of peas. Serve warm.

Coconut Shrimp

WITH SPICY ORANGE SAUCE

24   large shrimp, peeled, deveined,
        and butterflied, tail on

⅓   cup cornstarch or potato starch
½   teaspoon sea or kosher salt
¼   teaspoon ground pepper
¼   teaspoon cayenne pepper

2   large egg whites

2   cups (about 7 ounces) shredded
        sweetened coconut

Vegetable oil for frying

SPICY ORANGE SAUCE
½   cup orange marmalade
2   teaspoons stone-ground mustard
1   teaspoon prepared horseradish
        or ½ teaspoon red wine vinegar
Few dashes of ground pepper
Dash of salt

This is based on a recipe by Alton Brown. The picture to the right shows me making this dish at one of my cooking classes. It was a big hit!

Serves 4-6

1. Get 2 medium bowls ready and 1 shallow dish. In the first bowl, combine cornstarch, salt, pepper, and cayenne. In a second bowl, whisk egg whites until foamy. In the shallow dish, place the coconut.
2. Pat the shrimp dry. Holding the shrimp by the tail, coat shrimp with cornstarch first and shake off excess. Dip into egg white and then place in coconut. Press the shrimp into the coconut to make sure it's all covered. Batter at least half the shrimp and then proceed to next step. Batter the remaining shrimp while the first batch is cooking.
3. Place enough oil to generously cover the bottom of a large pan. Heat pan over medium to medium high heat. When the oil is hot, carefully place shrimp in the pan. Do not overcrowd the pan; you will probably have to fry them in 2-3 batches. Fry until golden brown on each side and firm, about 3-4 minutes per side. Remove and place on a plate lined with 1 or 2 pieces of paper towel; this will help to absorb some of the oil.
4. For the sauce, mix marmalade, mustard, horseradish or vinegar, pepper, and salt in a small bowl.
5. Serve immediately. If shrimp have gotten cold and/or soggy, re-heat in a 375°F oven for 5-8 minutes or until hot and crisp.

Pan-Grilled Fish

¼　teaspoon sea or kosher salt
⅛　teaspoon ground pepper
1　pound fish, like petrale sole, swordfish, halibut, or tilapia
2　teaspoons olive oil

Cooking fish is fairly easy if you keep it simple. One of my testers said," This is a great meal to whip up when you want to feel like you're eating something a little fancier than the standard fare but maybe don't have a lot of prep time."

Serves 3-4

1. Season the fish with salt and pepper.
2. Heat a non-stick pan with the oil over medium heat until hot. Carefully place fish down so as not to splatter the oil and burn yourself. Do not move the fish in the pan.
3. After the fish has been cooking about 3-5 minutes, carefully turn over and lower heat. Cook about another 2 minutes.
4. Allow to rest and serve.

Chef Tip

You can also change the seasonings (see *Flavor Profile Variations for Seasonings* in the Index) to make other types of dishes. For example, you can use the Mexican seasoning to make fish tacos.

Lemon Caper Sauce

Juice of 1-2 lemons (start with 1 lemon and add the other only if you need it)
1　garlic clove, minced
½-1　teaspoon kosher or sea salt
2-3　teaspoons of capers, drained
4-8　tablespoons unsalted butter

This sauce was created by my neighbors' daughters when they were about 8 and 10 years old. I adapted it somewhat and felt it had to be included. It is not only naturally gluten-free, but it's so good as well. It will go nicely with seafood, especially white fish, salmon, or shrimp. You can also serve it with chicken, pasta, rice, or tofu. One tester's young son loved it with his broccoli and wanted it to be a new sauce for his hot dogs!

Makes 4-6 servings of sauce

Add juice of 1 lemon, garlic, capers, and salt to a small pot. Bring to a simmer. Add butter, 1 tablespoon at a time, and whisk until melted. Add enough butter to taste or until the sauce is creamy and slightly thickened. Do not overstir; the butter will "break" and the sauce will no longer be creamy.

If you want less fat and more sauce, add broth (vegetable or chicken) and thicken with cornstarch if necessary. See *Making Sauces and Gravies* (see Index) for instructions.

Contents

Grains and Side Dishes

When I first went gluten-free, my attitude was to think about what you *can* have instead of what you *can't* have. That is about the time I discovered a number of grains I had never used before, like quinoa and millet. Being Italian, I have always made risotto so I had to give you my favorite recipes. I started making more polenta, which I realized I loved. Well, as you see with the rest of the dishes, I have converted a number of favorites such as cornbread and popovers. The other dishes are ones that I thought you would appreciate.

The photo of the Thanksgiving plate, in the Holiday Sides section, is an actual photo of my dish at my sister's house, taken in 2011. Just like many families, this was a blended meal with gluten and gluten-free. We had two stuffings, two pumpkin pies, and two sets of dinner rolls. However, my gluten-free gravy stood its ground; everyone loved it. It proved that yes, you can have a holiday meal that does not feel like you are being deprived. I have included recipes for almost everything you see in that photo.

The dishes in this chapter are perfect for your own family meals or for bringing to a friend's house. I hope you enjoy them as much as we do.

See the *Stocking the Pantry* and *Common Substitutions* chapters for more information on gluten-free ingredients, substitutions, and instructions for making *Amy's Gluten-Free Flour Blend*. Always check ingredients to make sure they are gluten-free.

Amaranth

Arborio rice (for risotto)

Red quinoa

Millet

Cooking Grains

In order to give your body different types of nutrients, it's important to eat different grains. Most people associate whole grains with whole wheat. When you are on a gluten-free diet, it's the perfect time to start exploring some other ones. However, grains (or anything) from the bulk aisle can be contaminated with gluten from other bins. If you have celiac disease or are gluten intolerant, buy grains from a package.

Try some of the following grains, using the ratios below. You can use water or broth for the liquid. For example, cook 1 cup of quinoa with 2 cups of water or broth.

All grains should be rinsed first using a mesh strainer and cooked with a dash of salt for flavor.

ITEM	RATIO OF LIQUID TO ITEM	HOW TO COOK
QUINOA	2:1	Place rinsed quinoa, water, and salt in a pot, and bring to boil. Cover, lower to simmer, cook 12-15 minutes or until water is absorbed.
MILLET	2.5:1	Place rinsed millet, water, and salt in a pot, and bring to boil. Cover, lower to simmer, cook 15-20 minutes or until water is absorbed.
BUCKWHEAT/KASHA*	2:1	Bring water and salt to a boil in a pot. Add rinsed buckwheat, stir, and cover. Lower to a simmer and cook 15 minutes. Remove from heat and let rest 10 minutes.
AMARANTH	2.5:1	Bring water and salt to a boil in a pot. Add rinsed amaranth. Turn heat down to low, cover, and cook 12-15 minutes.
BROWN RICE	2.25:1	Bring water and salt to a boil in a pot. Add rice. Turn heat down to low, cover, and cook 35-45 minutes.

*Note: If you are gluten intolerant, make sure the buckwheat is certified gluten-free as some buckwheat can contain gluten from cross-contamination.

IDEAS FOR USING GRAINS IN COOKING:

- When cooking rice, replace some of the rice with quinoa (about 1/3). For example, use 1 cup jasmine rice, ½ cup red quinoa and 3 cups of water.
- Add cooked millet or quinoa to mashed white or sweet potatoes, use as a base for stew, or serve instead of rice with a little butter and salt.
- Serve cooked kasha with a stew-type dish, use in place of bread cubes in stuffing, or serve with a mushroom sauce.
- Grind grains in a clean coffee grinder and use like oats for breakfast. Bring 1 cup of water to a boil and add 1/3 cup ground grains. Cook about 10 minutes.
- Use brown rice when making Mexican rice, use as a base in a casserole, or add to soup.

Sweet Potato Millet Cakes

2-3 medium sized sweet potatoes
½ cup millet, rinsed
2 teaspoons olive oil
1 onion, chopped
1½ teaspoons kosher or sea salt
½ teaspoon each thyme, cumin, and curry powder
¼ teaspoon ground pepper

½ cup potato starch or *Amy's Gluten-Free Flour Blend*

Oil for frying like safflower or olive

CUMIN SCENTED CREAM
1 cup sour cream, yogurt, or mayonnaise (for dairy-free)
½ teaspoon sea or kosher salt
¼-½ teaspoon cumin

One of the grocery stores where I shop makes something like this which is sold in their prepared foods case. Although some of the ingredients are similar, I created my own version (theirs looks and tastes different).

Millet is not only good for you, it also has great flavor. It cooks up sort of "spongy" and is great to absorb something liquidy like a stew. You can usually find it in the rice or grain section of a natural foods store. If you can't find millet, use quinoa.

Use the potatoes with the red skin and orange interior. Regardless of what they are called, these are the ones which are best. Scrape a little of the skin to make sure you have the correct one. These potatoes are full of vitamins (A, B6, and C) and minerals (manganese, iron, and potassium). So, a "cake" made with both this and the millet is a double-whammy of nutrition. Try serving it with the cumin cream. Delish!

Makes 20-24 cakes

1. Wash potatoes well and prick with a fork or knife. Bake potatoes in a 400°F oven for about 45 minutes or until tender. Or, microwave for 3-4 minutes, rotating at least once, until tender. Cut potatoes open and cool slightly. Remove skins, place in bowl and mash. Cool completely. It's important that the potatoes are cool; otherwise the mixture could be too wet.
2. Cook millet. Add millet to 1¼ cups of water with a pinch of salt. Bring to a boil and lower to a simmer. Cover and cook 15-20 minutes or until water is absorbed.
3. Sauté the onion in olive oil with the salt and spices. Cook until the onion is soft and golden brown. Cool slightly.
4. Once the millet and onions have cooled, mix with the sweet potato and salt. Taste mixture and add more seasonings if necessary. If it seems very wet and you have extra millet, add between ½ to 1 cup more. Add potato starch and mix. Add more if necessary so that you can form the mix into patties.
5. Form into 2-3" patties. Cook over medium heat in a non-stick pan with oil until golden on each side (if you don't have a non-stick pan, make sure there is a layer of oil on the bottom and that the oil is hot before adding the patties). Alternatively, bake in a 400°F oven on a greased cookie sheet, for about 18-20 minutes, turning once.
6. Mix sour cream with salt and cumin. Serve a dollop on top of each cake.

Lentil and Rice Pilaf

3   cups low sodium chicken
or vegetable broth
⅓   cup brown lentils, rinsed
⅔   cup brown rice
1   pinch of saffron
½   cup frozen peas (optional)
1   tablespoon unsalted butter or good
quality olive oil (for dairy-free)
¼   teaspoon sea or kosher salt

Serves 4

1. Heat broth to boiling in a medium size pot. Add lentils, rice, and saffron. Stir, cover, and bring back to a boil. Lower to a simmer and cook 30-35 minutes.
2. Remove cover and stir, making sure it is not sticky and that there is still some liquid. If there is not, add ¼ cup more broth or water. Add frozen peas and stir. Place cover back on and raise heat to bring back to a simmer. Continue to cook until liquid is absorbed and lentils are cooked.
3. When the pilaf is done, add the butter or oil, salt, and then stir.

Mexican Brown Rice

2½   cups chicken or vegetable broth
(if using a rice cooker, you might
need to increase to 3 cups)
1   tablespoon unsalted butter
(for dairy-free, use a butter
substitute or olive oil)
1-2   tablespoons tomato paste
1   cup brown rice
½   medium onion, diced

On taco nights, when I don't feel like making a big meal but want some extra nutrition, I make this rice dish and serve it with beans.

In a medium sauce pan, bring chicken broth, tomato paste, and butter to a simmer. Add remaining ingredients and cook for 35-40 minutes or until the liquid has been absorbed. Let rest for 5 minutes before serving.

Tip: Wondering what to do with the rest of the can of tomato paste? Place in a freezer bag and close. Using your finger, make 3-4 indentations in the bag and freeze. When you need a tablespoon or so, break off a piece and defrost it. Genius!

Freeze leftover tomato paste in blocks in a plastic bag.

Beef Saffron Risotto

1-1¼ pounds ground beef or turkey
1 medium onion, diced (or ½ large)
¼ teaspoon ground pepper
2 pinches saffron
½ teaspoon sea or kosher salt
¼ cup cooking wine like sherry
or dry white wine
1 cup arborio rice
3½-4 cups of chicken broth,
heated to a simmer
1 cup frozen peas, slightly
thawed or chopped spinach
1 tablespoon unsalted butter or good
quality olive oil (for dairy-free)

Grated Italian cheese like pecorino romano, Parmesan, or locatelli

This dish was originally made by my Grandma Eleanor (my father's mother). She taught my mother how to make it and my mother taught me. It's a family favorite.

A Family Chef Signature Recipe!

You might not expect risotto in a gluten-free cookbook since it is naturally gluten-free but it is a dish many people are afraid to make at home. It has been a favorite in our family, in cooking classes, and for many guests in my home. The combination of flavors is unique and the end result is delicious.

I like this dish because it's easy to prepare, even on a weeknight. My mom made this for me when I was young, and now I make it for my children. The smell and taste of it brings back memories. I hope my children will say the same thing, and maybe yours will, too.

Serves 4

1. Heat large pot to medium. Make sure the pan is hot and add ground meat in small clumps, being careful not to overcrowd the pan (see Index for *Browning Ground Meat* for tips). After you have put the meat in the pan, do not stir it. Once it is brown on one side, turn over and cook until the other side is brown. Then, use a spoon to chop up the meat. If the meat is browned, the dish will be flavored better. Drain any extra fat and place the meat back in the pot.
2. Add onion, ground pepper, and saffron. Raise the heat a little and cook until the onion is translucent and the meat becomes a little more browned. Add salt and garlic; cook 1 minute.
3. Add the cooking wine and cook until it is evaporated, 1-2 minutes. Add rice and cook for 5-7 minutes, stirring. Rice should turn translucent.
4. Begin to add hot chicken broth, 1 cup at first. Stir every 2-3 minutes and add more broth after the last addition has been absorbed, about ½ to 1 cup at a time. Make sure rice is simmering but not boiling. Check after about 18 minutes or when the rice looks cooked. Taste rice; it should be slightly firm and not mushy. If you need more liquid and don't have broth, add hot water. You may need some broth at the end to loosen the risotto before serving.
5. Add peas and stir. Cook for 2 minutes and shut the heat off. Add butter or oil.
6. Stir before serving; add more broth if it is thick. Taste and season with salt and pepper if needed. Garnish risotto with grated cheese.

Polenta

4½   cups water
2   teaspoons sea or kosher salt
1½   cups polenta (coarse cornmeal)
½   cup grated Italian cheese
       (if you omit, add at least ½
       teaspoon of extra salt)
2   tablespoons olive oil or butter
Rounded ¼ teaspoon ground pepper

**OPTIONAL: few dashes of
crushed red chile pepper**

Using polenta for lasagna offers a variety of options from gluten-free to dairy-free to vegan (just omit cheeses!). It's all about the process. You can use the recipe below to make Polenta Lasagna right away or, with the Make-Ahead version, use it to make the polenta first and then use it more like a noodle after it has cooled.

Serves 4-6

MASTER POLENTA RECIPE

1. Bring water to a boil in a medium to large pot. Add salt. While water is boiling, slowly add polenta in a steady stream, whisking constantly.
2. Add cheese, oil or butter, and seasonings. Lower heat and simmer until thickened, stirring every few minutes. If bubbling hard, lower the heat.
3. Cook for 18-20 minutes. Polenta is done when it is thick and pulling away from the side of the pan. Remove pan from heat. See recipe on the next page for further instructions.

MAKE-AHEAD VERSION

Follow directions above. Once polenta is thick and pulling away from the sides of the pan, pour into 2 greased 13" × 9" pans (or any pan which will make the polenta flat) and spread with a rubber spatula. Cool completely. Remove from pans and cut each piece into 4 pieces (approximately ½" × 3" × 9") to give you a total of 8 pieces. Lay these out as your would lasagna noodles. See recipe on the following page.

Chef Tip

When making polenta for lasagna, it needs to be firm, so use a ratio of 3 parts water to 1 part polenta or coarse cornmeal. It's easy to make more or less, depending upon the size pan you have. You can also use a variety of fillings and sauces. Be creative and have fun!

Polenta Lasagna

TRADITIONAL

1 recipe Master Polenta
(see prior page)
1 recipe ricotta filling
2-3 cups tomato sauce (see Index)
1 cup shredded mozzarella

RICOTTA FILLING
1 egg
1 pound whole milk ricotta
½ cup grated Parmesan cheese
½ cup shredded mozzarella cheese
½ cup milk
1 teaspoon sea or kosher salt
½ teaspoon ground pepper
½ teaspoon garlic powder

OPTIONAL
10 ounces frozen chopped
spinach, thawed and drained

Make sure to read this recipe through first. I would suggest starting with the polenta. While that cooks, prepare the ricotta filling and shred the mozzarella. It's important to work quickly once the polenta is done; otherwise it will be too hard to spread.

Serves 6-8

1. Preheat oven to 375°F. Grease a 13" × 9" pan.
2. While the polenta cooks, mix ricotta filling ingredients in a medium bowl and set aside. Optionally, add the spinach to the filling.
3. When the polenta is cooked, pour half of it into the pan and spread. Be careful not to spread more than half; otherwise you won't have enough for the top. If you are using the pre-cooked polenta, fit it into the pan. Place 1 cup of tomato sauce on top and spread to cover polenta. Top with the ricotta filling and spread evenly.
4. Top with remaining polenta and spread (or fit lasagna pieces). If the polenta is stiff, try using a spatula dipped in hot water to help spread evenly or use 2 spatulas. Top with 1 cup of tomato sauce. Cover with greased foil (grease the part that will touch the sauce; otherwise it will stick.
5. Bake lasagna until bubbly, about 25-30 minutes.
6. Remove foil and place cheese on top. Bake an additional 5-10 minutes or until cheese is melted.
7. Remove lasagna from oven. Let rest for 10-15 minutes before serving. Optionally serve with additional tomato sauce.

---

4 cups assorted vegetables, chopped
in bite size pieces, for example:
onion, pepper, zucchini, broccoli,
cauliflower, cherry tomatoes,
eggplant, sweet potatoes, etc.
1-2 tablespoons olive oil
1 teaspoon sea or kosher salt
¼ teaspoon ground pepper
½-1 teaspoon other seasonings like
thyme, rosemary, basil, oregano,
and garlic powder (or 2 cloves
of minced fresh garlic)
1 recipe Master Polenta
(see prior page)
8 ounces crumbled gorgonzola
or bleu cheese
2-3 thinly sliced tomatoes (patted dry)

VARIATION: POLENTA LASAGNA WITH ROASTED VEGETABLES AND GORGONZOLA

1. Place veggies in a bowl with oil and seasonings and toss. Place in roasting pan and bake in a 375°F oven for about 15-20 minutes or until softened, stirring once. Cool slightly.
2. Preheat oven to 375°F. Grease a 13" × 9" dish.
3. When polenta is cooked, pour half into a greased baking pan. Top with roasted vegetables and half of the gorgonzola or bleu cheese. Spread remaining polenta on top.
4. Top with tomato slices and sprinkle salt on top.
5. Bake for 25 minutes. Add the remaining cheese. Bake an additional 10-15 minutes. Let rest for 10-15 minutes before serving.

Roasted Tomatoes

WITH POLENTA AND MASCARPONE CHEESE

2	pounds ripe plum tomatoes, cut in half lengthwise
2	tablespoons olive oil
2	teaspoons sea or kosher salt
¼	teaspoon ground pepper
1	teaspoon herbs de Provence
1	recipe Master Polenta (see prior page)
2	cloves fresh garlic, minced
6	ounces mascarpone cheese, softened
½	teaspoon sea or kosher salt
2	tablespoons packed basil, chopped (don't chop until ready to serve)

This is the perfect summer dish when tomatoes are at their peak. In the winter, you could make this with a thick tomato sauce.

1. Preheat oven to 375°F.
2. Place tomatoes in a bowl with oil and seasonings and toss.
3. Place in roasting pan and bake about 18-20 minutes or until softened and browned, stirring once.
4. While the tomatoes are roasting, make the polenta and pour into a greased 13" × 9" baking pan. Cool. Top polenta with mascarpone cheese. Sprinkle salt on top.
5. Add garlic to the roasted tomatoes and cook 3 more minutes.
6. Remove the tomatoes from oven and pour on top of the polenta, spreading evenly.
7. Top with chopped basil and cut into squares.

Polenta Lasagna

Roasted Tomatoes over Polenta

How to Cook a Gluten-Free Holiday Meal

The photo to the left is my dinner plate from our meal at my sister's house in 2011. When I am with my extended family, only half of us eat gluten-free. Since I tend to do most of the cooking, rather than making two versions of each dish, I make dishes that are delicious and gluten-free. This way, no one feels denied. I have to say, this was a tasty meal! Sure, they had their own stuffing and pie but we were very happy with ours.

Here are my suggestions for a gluten-free holiday meal everyone will enjoy. With the exception of the roast turkey, you can find these recipes in this book. Check the Index.

Holiday Menu

Sweet Potato Millet Cakes

Corn Chowder with Chopped Bacon and Chives

Caesar Salad

—✲—

Roast Turkey (check brining ingredients for gluten if using)

Simple Gravy

Mashed Potatoes

Bread Stuffing

Creamed Spinach

Cornbread

Popovers

Cranberry Sauce

—✲—

Pumpkin Pie

Fruit Galette

Chocolate Brownies with Ganache

Bread Stuffing

1   **tablespoon olive or vegetable oil**
1   **medium onion, diced**
2   **celery ribs, diced**
1   **teaspoon dried thyme**
1   **teaspoon dried rosemary**
1   **teaspoon dried sage or poultry seasoning**
½   **teaspoon ground pepper**
½   **teaspoon sea or kosher salt**
1-2   **garlic cloves, chopped**
½   **cup water**
3-4   **cups gluten free croutons (see below)**
3-4   **cups chicken or vegetable broth**

OPTIONAL INGREDIENTS:
½   **cup nuts, lightly toasted and chopped**
2   **Italian sausages, cooked and crumbled**
½   **cup dried fruit like cranberry or raisins**

I can't believe how many years I went without stuffing! If you have your own recipe for stuffing, follow the steps below but use your own ingredients.
"You have made me one thankful mama this Thanksgiving day! Stuffing is one of those things that I've really missed since going gluten-free."–tester

Serves 6-8

1. Heat olive oil in a large sauté pan. Add onions, celery, thyme, rosemary, sage, and pepper. Without stirring too often, allow to cook until the celery is softened and the onions are golden. Add a little bit of salt if the vegetables seem dry.
2. Once vegetables are golden and softened, add garlic and salt. Cook for 1 minute. Add water and cook for 3-5 minutes or until most of it is evaporated.
3. Remove from pot and place in large mixing bowl. Cool for 5 minutes.
4. Preheat oven to 350°F.
5. Place all remaining ingredients except broth in the large bowl. Mix well. Add broth, 1 cup at a time, until the stuffing is moist.
6. Place stuffing in a greased medium to large baking dish and cover with foil. Bake for 20 minutes. Remove cover and bake until the top is lightly browned and crusty, about another 10 minutes.

Croutons

Makes about 3-4 cups

1-1½ **loaves of gluten-free sandwich bread, cut into cubes**
About 2-3 tablespoons olive oil
Kosher salt, ground pepper, dried oregano, and thyme (¼ – ½ teaspoon each)

Toss bread with olive oil and seasonings. Bake in a 400°F oven until lightly browned and crisp, about 8 minutes, stirring once. Cool.

Popovers

1   **cup *Amy's Gluten-Free Flour Blend***
¼   **teaspoon xanthan gum**
½   **teaspoon sea or kosher salt**

4   **large eggs**
1¼ **cups milk or milk substitute (plain and unsweetened), slightly warm**
3   **tablespoons unsalted butter or butter substitute, melted**

One of my testers loves this recipe so much, she makes it for her family for breakfast! This is adapted from a recipe from the website of King Arthur flour.

Makes 12 popovers

1. Preheat the oven to 400°F. Generously grease a 12-cup popover pan or muffin pan. Do not add liners.
2. In a small bowl, mix the flour blend, xanthan gum, and salt. Set aside.
3. In a blender, add eggs, milk, and butter. Mix on medium speed until the mixture is well blended. Add the dry ingredients to the blender and blend at medium-high speed until batter is smooth. If you see big lumps, blend again. Small ones are fine. Alternatively, you can do this process in a large bowl with a whisk until you have a smooth batter.
4. Pour the batter into the prepared pan, filling each cup about ⅔ full.
5. Bake for 20 minutes, then reduce the oven heat to 350°F and bake for an additional 10 minutes, until the popovers are deep brown.
6. Remove from the oven and let popovers rest for 5 minutes to finish setting. Remove from the pan and serve immediately.

Creamed Spinach

2   teaspoons olive oil
½   onion, diced
¼   teaspoon ground pepper
¼   teaspoon garlic powder
¼   teaspoon dry mustard
Sprinkle of nutmeg
1   10-ounce box frozen chopped
       spinach, thawed, and squeezed dry
½-1   teaspoon sea or kosher salt
2   cups milk or milk substitute,
       plain and unsweetened

SLURRY
Mix 2 tablespoons cornstarch with
2 tablespoons cold water

OPTIONAL
1-2 tablespoons nutritional yeast

Serves 3-4

1. Heat medium sized pot to medium. Add olive oil, onions, pepper, garlic powder, mustard, and nutmeg until translucent and golden. Add spinach and salt and cook for 2-3 minutes.
2. Add milk or milk substitute and bring almost to a simmer.
3. Mix slurry and add slowly to the sauce. Cook for 2 minutes, stirring. Continue to cook on a medium-low heat until thickened, stirring frequently. If sauce hasn't thickened after 5 minutes, make more slurry and repeat.
Note: for more information on *How to Make a Slurry*, see Index.
4. Check for seasonings. Optionally, add nutritional yeast to give it a cheese flavor without adding dairy.

Note: Nutritional yeast can be found in most health food/organic stores.

Mashed Potatoes with Variations

1½ pounds (about 5 or 6) russett potatoes, washed, peeled, and cut in quarters (you can optionally leave the skin on if you are short on time; just make sure to wash well)
3   teaspoons sea or kosher salt, divided
½   cup milk (whole works best, but you can use any type)
4   tablespoons unsalted butter
½   teaspoon white or black pepper

There's nothing like a good mashed potato recipe. We tend to like mashed with our meals so I thought it would be appropriate to provide a recipe with variations. The cauliflower and millet versions provide some extra nutrition along with great flavor; my children don't notice the additions. My rule of thumb, unless the potatoes are very large, is 1 potato per person and 1/2 of a potato per child. If I want leftovers, I use more.

Serves 4-6

MASTER MASHED POTATOES
1. In a large pot, cover potatoes with water. Add 2 teaspoons of salt and cover. Bring to boil and lower to a simmer.
2. Cook until fork-tender and drain, leaving a little liquid in the pot.
3. To the drained potatoes, add remaining ingredients except salt and mash well with a potato masher. To make extra fluffy, whip with a circular motion using the masher, or blend with a hand mixer. Taste for seasonings and add more salt or pepper if needed.

DAIRY-FREE/VEGAN MASHED POTATOES
Follow directions for recipe above. Use milk substitute, plain and unsweetened, instead of regular milk. Use butter substitute or olive oil for the butter.

MILLET MASHED POTATOES
1. Add ½ cup of rinsed millet to 1¼ cups of water with a pinch of salt to a medium pot. Bring to a boil and then lower to a simmer and cover. Cook about 20 minutes or until all of the water has been absorbed.
2. Follow directions for either recipe above. Fold in cooked millet at the end.

CAULIFLOWER MASHED POTATOES
Follow directions for either recipe above except replace 2 potatoes with ½ head of cauliflower, chopped into small pieces. Make sure cauliflower is also soft before you mash the potatoes.

Cranberry Sauce

¾ cup water or orange juice (use ¼ cup less sugar if using the juice)
⅓ cup white sugar
⅓ cup agave nectar, honey, or sugar

4 cups (12-ounce package) fresh or frozen cranberries, rinsed

OPTIONAL INGREDIENTS:
½ cup toasted pecans or walnuts, chopped
Orange zest from ½ of an orange
¾ cup raisins or currants
¼ teaspoon of cinnamon, nutmeg, or allspice

It's easy to make your own fresh cranberry sauce with just a few ingredients. This version has much less sugar than what you would find in a can. Give it a try. If you don't think you'll use all of the cranberries, cut the recipe in half and use the berries in a muffin or loaf. You can use the Blueberry Muffin recipe (see Index) and substitute cranberries for blueberries.

Makes 8-10 servings

1. Place water, sugar, and agave nectar in a small to medium saucepan over medium heat. Bring to a boil, stirring to dissolve sugar.
2. Add cranberries and return to a boil. Reduce heat and simmer for 10 minutes or until cranberries burst. At the end, add any of the optional ingredients.
3. Remove from heat. Cool completely at room temperature and then chill in refrigerator. Cranberry sauce will thicken as it cools.

Potato Latkes

1   **onion**
2   **pounds potatoes, peeled**
1   **egg**
1   **teaspoon kosher salt**
¼   **teaspoon baking powder**
2   **tablespoons *Amy's Gluten-Free Flour Blend***
1   **tablespoon cornstarch or potato starch**
Oil for frying, for example vegetable shortening, vegetable oil, or peanut oil

OPTIONAL FOR GARNISH:
Apple sauce
Sour cream

Traditional latkes are made with flour and/or matzoh. When you talk to someone who is Jewish about latke-making, it can be a serious and personal subject. My good friend Dayna shared her recipe, which is really proportions, and I managed to convert it to gluten-free. I don't make them very often but when I do, the plate is empty at the end of the meal.

1. In a food processor, puree the onion. Squeeze in a cloth to remove the excess water. Set aside. If you are going to use a food processor to shred the potatoes, you only need to rinse out the bowl.
2. Shred the peeled potatoes and squeeze in a cloth to remove the excess water.
3. In a large bowl, add egg, salt, baking powder, flour blend and corn or potato starch. Mix together. Add potatoes and onion to make the batter.
4. Heat a large pan with enough oil to cover the bottom over medium-high heat. When the oil is hot, form the batter into 2"-3" flat patties and carefully place in pan. Be careful not to crowd the pan or else it won't brown.
5. Use long tongs or a spatula to turn over when the latkes are brown on one side. They will cook quickly in the hot oil.
6. Place on a large dish or tray lined with paper towels.
7. Top with kosher salt if they taste a little "flat". Serve hot with apple-sauce and sour cream.

Sautéed Dino Kale with White Beans

1 pound gluten-free pasta like rotini or small shells
1 tablespoon sea or kosher salt, divided
1 bunch dinosaur kale (also known as Lacinato kale; you can use almost any type)
1 medium onion, finely chopped
1-2 garlic cloves, chopped
1 tablespoon olive oil
¼ teaspoon ground pepper
1 can cannellini or white kidney beans, drained and rinsed

Freshly grated Parmesan cheese
Extra virgin olive oil

When my friend Amy Andrews of Amy's Food Room posted this on her blog, I thought, "My kids will never eat that!" However, realizing I should follow my own advice of never assuming what kids will and won't eat, I decided to make it. Of course, they loved it. It's been a favorite at home and in cooking classes. We serve it with quinoa pasta shells and freshly grated Parmesan cheese.

Makes 4 servings

1. Cook pasta. Review the *Gluten-Free Pasta Cooking Tips* (see Index) for more information. Prep the kale and onions while the pasta cooks. Once the pasta is cooked, drain and keep warm.
2. Cut the bottom of the stems of kale (I usually cut at the rubber band or wire wrapper). Remove middle stalk which is quite tough. Placing 2-3 on top of one another, first cut into 2-3 long strips and then cut into 1" pieces, cutting the opposite direction of the long leaf.
3. Place the kale pieces in a large bowl with cold water. Move them around a bit to remove any dirt from the leaves and do not remove from water yet. Set aside.
4. Heat a large sauté pan over medium heat, then add olive oil, onion, and ground pepper. Cook for a few minutes, only stirring occasionally, until onions just start to brown. Add garlic and remaining teaspoon of salt; cook 1 minute.
5. With your hands, pick up kale leaves from the bowl of water and place in the pan. Do not drain as the dirt may stay on the leaves. Cover with a lid (it doesn't have to fit tightly, you just want something to keep some of the moisture in). Every few minutes, give the greens a toss or stir. Taste and add more salt and pepper if needed.
6. Add beans and stir. Cook until beans are heated through.
7. In a large bowl, add cooked pasta and toss. Garnish with cheese and extra virgin olive oil.

Zucchini Pancakes

Makes 15-20 pancakes

2-3   zucchinis (see step 1)
¼-½ teaspoons sea or kosher salt

Olive oil for sautéing
½   onion, chopped or sliced thinly

1   large egg, beaten
¼   teaspoon ground pepper
Optional seasonings: ¼ teaspoon
    of each-dried dill, thyme
    and/or oregano

¼   cup *Amy's Gluten-Free Flour Blend*,
    potato starch or cornstarch

1. Shred the zucchini with the skin on with a food processor, mandoline or a metal box grater. You should have about 2 cups in total. Place in a mesh strainer over a bowl. Sprinkle salt over zucchini (at least ¼ teaspoon) and mix. Let sit for at least 15 minutes while you prep the other ingredients.
2. Sauté onion in about 1-2 teaspoons of olive oil until just softened. The onion is optional but gives the pancakes good flavor. By cooking them first, they are sweeter and less strong-flavored. Once cooked, place in a medium to large bowl to cool.
3. Remove the liquid from the zucchini by pressing it against the strainer or wringing it in a kitchen towel. Place in the bowl with the onion. Add the egg and pepper and mix with either a spoon or your hands. If you are using any optional seasonings, add them now.
4. Add the flour mixture or starch, 1 tablespoon at a time until the mixture is moist but not runny. You should be able to make pancakes that will keep their shape. You may not use all of the flour. Shape 2" pancakes and place on a plate until you are ready to cook them.
5. Heat a non-stick griddle or sauté pan. Spray with non-stick spray or use 1 teaspoon of olive oil. If you are not using a non-stick pan, you will need to use more oil or else the pancakes will stick.
6. Place pancakes on pan and flatten out slightly. Cook about 4-5 minutes on each side or until golden brown. Serve plain or with herbed cream.

Fresh Herbed Cream

Makes 2 cups

1½ cups sour cream or crème fraiche
    (for dairy-free, use mayonnaise
    or a dairy-free plain yogurt)
2   tablespoons chopped parsley
1   teaspoon each chopped fresh
    dill, oregano, and thyme
    (or ½ teaspoon dried)
½   teaspoon sea or kosher salt
1   medium garlic clove, minced
¼   teaspoon ground pepper
1   tablespoon white vinegar
    or lemon juice

Mix all ingredients. Place in the fridge and wait 30 minutes before using.

Contents

Breads, Pizza, and More

When I think of a warm kitchen, I picture a warm loaf of bread coming out of the oven. Many people who are on a gluten-free diet think they will never have good bread again. I'm here to tell you that you can make gluten-free bread, pizza, and biscuits successfully! I put a lot of details into the recipes so that you would feel confident to try them yourself. One of my keys to success is simplifying the recipes by using only one flour blend (with a few exceptions).

When I first made gluten-free baked goods, I found the process of measuring the flours tiresome. When I started to experiment with the concept of a single flour blend, the result was a basic white flour blend. If I want more of a whole grain texture, I make a few simple additions of other flours. The switch to a single flour blend as the basis for my baking saves time and still tastes great.

My family really missed pizza, so I experimented with many different recipes to find the perfect dough. I've provided two here; one featuring a soft and chewy crust and one that is crispier. I have also included recipes for bagels, cornbread, biscuits, and cheese crackers.

If you are either tired of paying a lot for store-bought gluten-free bread or depriving yourself entirely of bread, give these recipes a try. You will see a notable difference in quality over purchased baked goods. Tasting fresh bread or pizza as it comes out of the oven…well, it's that little slice of heaven which makes it all worth it.

See the *Stocking the Pantry* and *Common Substitutions* chapters for more information on gluten-free ingredients, substitutions, and instructions for making *Amy's Gluten-Free Flour Blend*. Always check ingredients to make sure they are gluten-free.

Quick rising yeast is usually added to the dry ingredients.

Bread made in a bread machine.

Use an instant read thermometer to determine the temperature of the liquid.

Gluten-Free Yeast Breads

One thing I really miss being on a gluten-free diet is bread. There just is no denying it. But one benefit of cooking for more than 20 years (half of that time in commercial kitchens), is that I am very comfortable in the kitchen changing recipes until the end result is exactly what I want.

I made bread in the bread machine for a number of years with great results. When I started cooking gluten-free almost 5 years ago, I noticed that every recipe seemed very complicated, even to me. It took me 10 minutes to just measure out all of the flours. I've adapted most of my old favorite recipes to include just my flour blend with a few exceptions.

When I do change the flour, it's to make a variation like whole grain or "rye." I keep the process the same, so it's easy for you to vary the recipes. You will find it much easier to create your own variations if you would like.

Another obstacle for many people when baking gluten-free is yeast. Don't be scared! It's actually very easy. Even some of my testers who never baked bread before, said they found these recipes to be very straightforward.

Take a few minutes to familiarize yourself with these tips below. These will help you in your baking and also with conversions.

Tips for Baking Products with Yeast

INGREDIENTS

Liquid: Generally the liquid in any of these recipes calls for water, milk, or both. I have found you can just use water, so it's easy to make the dish dairy-free.

Temperature of the liquid: I would invest in an instant read thermometer, pictured to the left. For less than $10, this thermometer measures the temperature of your liquid. The reason it's important is the yeast. If it's too hot or not warm enough, the yeast will die and the bread won't rise.

- **Active Dry Yeast** (I refer to as "regular"): the liquid should be between 105°F-115°F or warm.
- **Quick or Rapid Rise Yeast** (I refer to as "quick"): the liquid should be between 120°F-130°F or hot.

Yeast: Yeast needs 3 things in order to grow: moisture or liquid, food (usually sugar but this can be flour), and warmth (a little warmer than room temperature). Proofing the dry yeast is done to make sure the yeast is active. That means you put it in warm water (moisture and warmth) with some sugar (food) to make sure it is alive. It will be bubbly, fragrant, and foamy in 5 minutes if it's alive. This proofed yeast mixture is usually added with other wet or liquid ingredients. If it doesn't foam up, start over.

Most yeast today, if used before its expiration date, is probably active. Maybe it is habit or maybe it's the smell; but I still proof my regular yeast. I tend to add the quick rising yeast to the dry ingredients. Do what you are comfortable with, but don't be afraid to use recipes with yeast! The less than $10 thermometer is your friend.

When you make bread with regular yeast, the dough takes about 60 minutes to rise. If you use quick rising or rapid yeast, that time is cut by a third; taking only 20 minutes.

Sugar: The sugar helps the yeast to thrive and gives the bread nice flavor as well. Most of the sugar in the bread recipes can be reduced.

Vinegar: Vinegar helps to make the yeast more active which helps in the rise, adds taste and texture, and acts as a natural preservative. I use white vinegar or apple cider vinegar. Never use malt vinegar since it has gluten in it.

Ground ginger: I almost always add ⅛ teaspoon of this to my breads since it's another natural preservative. My bread can last 2-3 days longer when I add the ginger. I highly recommend it.

Eggs: Eggs help with the texture and rise as well as the color. If you want it to be less yellow, use only egg whites. If the recipe calls for 2 eggs, use 3 egg whites. Eggs should be at room temperature. See the tip to the right if your eggs are cold.

Egg Substitute: For egg-free baking, review the *Substitutions* chapter (see Index). Flax seed and water is a good substitute in bread.

Oil: Oils or fats help to create a bread that is moist, chewier, and more flavorful. I tend to use olive oil, but you can use any mild-flavored vegetable oil. I would not recommend sesame oil.

Xanthan Gum: Oh, we can't forget our friend xanthan gum when making bread! It really helps to hold it together. Normally my ratio is ½ teaspoon xanthan for every 2 cups of gluten-free flour. For bread and pizza, it's much higher. The gum helps with the chew and helps the bread stay together. If you have guar gum, review the *Substitutions* chapter (see Index).

A container of gluten-free flour is handy for baking.

It's easiest if all ingredients are measured before you start.

Place cold eggs in a bowl with hot water for 5 minutes to bring to room temperature quickly.

When baking bread, the technique is always the same…

There are many different combinations of gluten-free bread baking. Use the tips below. The first recipe for white bread is the master recipe for technique. After that, the following recipes are all variations of the first. By changing out the flours and/or liquids and adding extra ingredients, *White Bread* can become *Whole Grain*, *"Rye"*, or *Cinnamon Raisin*.

| Bread Machine

Bread Machine vs Stand Mixer

BREAD MACHINE: Follow the manufacturer's directions for the type of yeast that you have (quick usually takes 60 minutes total; regular takes 2-3 hours). Select a large loaf. Some bread machines now have gluten-free settings. After a few minutes of mixing, scrape the corners of the bowl as the flour can get stuck there. If you can, once the machine stops mixing, remove the paddle so there is no hole in the bottom of the bread.

| Stand Mixer

STAND MIXER AND OVEN: I would recommend using a stand mixer because the dough is very stiff and sticky. However you can try mixing by hand or with a powerful hand mixer.
You may need to use two loaf pans when baking the bread; check the recipe for the dimensions.
Most breads take 30-35 minutes when baked at 350°F. Judge the doneness by the color and smell.

PROOFING (RISING) OF THE BREAD
When you make bread in a stand mixer, regardless of the yeast that you use, one of the steps is the proofing or rising of the bread, which is different than proofing of the yeast. Yeast breads need to rise in a warm place, 80°F-90°F. If the room where you are baking is not that warm, turn the oven on to a low temperature, for example 200°F, for about 3-5 minutes. Shut the oven off before placing the dough in the oven to rise.

| Rising of the Bread

When you use the bread machine, the rising takes place in the bread machine itself.

How To Make It...

MAKING BREAD WITH QUICK RISING YEAST IN A BREAD MACHINE

What you need to know:
This is the easiest and quickest way to make delicious gluten-free bread.

1. Mix quick rising yeast with the dry ingredients in a medium bowl.

2. Add liquid ingredients to bowl of bread machine.

3. Add dry ingredients.

4. Turn on bread machine and select appropriate setting.

5. Scrape the corners to incorporate the flour.

How To Make It...

MAKING BREAD WITH QUICK RISING YEAST IN A STAND MIXER

1. Add quick rising yeast with the dry ingredients in the stand mixer bowl.

2. Add liquid ingredients to the bowl and mix for 2-3 minutes until stiff and glossy.

3. Spread into greased loaf pans and allow to rise 25-30 minutes.

4. Bake 30-35 minutes.

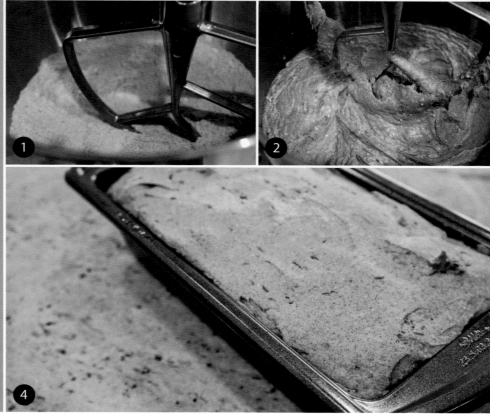

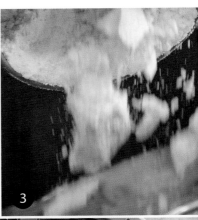

How To Make It...

MAKING BREAD WITH REGULAR YEAST IN A BREAD MACHINE

What you need to know:

Baking bread with regular yeast in a bread machine takes about 3 hours.

In my experience, bread rises better in the bread machine when I use quick rising yeast.

1. Add warm liquid, yeast, and sugar to bread machine bowl.

2. Mix dry ingredients in a medium bowl.

3. Add remaining liquid ingredients to bread machine. Carefully add dry ingredients.

4. Turn on bread machine and select appropriate setting.

5. Scrape the corners to incorporate the flour.

6. Remove bread from pan at the end of the baking cycle.

How To Make It...

MAKING BREAD WITH REGULAR YEAST IN A STAND MIXER

What you need to know:

Proof the regular yeast first.
You can make 1 or 2 loaves depending upon the size of the loaf pan.
This method takes the most time but works if you don't have a bread machine.

1 Proof yeast with warm liquid and sugar. Set aside for 5 minutes. Have the other liquid ingredients ready to go in another bowl.

2 Add the dry ingredients to the stand mixer bowl and mix.

3 Add liquid ingredients, including yeast mixture, to the bowl and mix for 2-3 minutes until stiff and glossy.

4 Spread into greased loaf pan(s).

5 Proof dough in a warm place to rise until almost doubled. Bake 30-35 minutes.

Everyday White Bread with Regular Yeast

1   cup water
½   cup milk or milk substitute, plain
       and unsweetened (you can use
       all water instead of milk)
2¼   teaspoons regular or
       active yeast (1 packet)
1   teaspoon sugar (always
       use for this method)

3¼   cups *Amy's Gluten-Free Flour Blend*
2   teaspoons xanthan gum
1   teaspoon sea or kosher salt
⅛   teaspoon ground ginger (optional)

2   large eggs, beaten, at
       room temperature
1   teaspoon apple cider
       vinegar or white vinegar
1½   tablespoons olive oil or
       vegetable oil like safflower
1   tablespoon honey or agave nectar

Chef Tips

You can use up to 1½ teaspoons of salt if you prefer. Use less if you only have table salt. This recipe fits in a 9¼" × 5¼" × 2¾" loaf pan. If your pan is smaller, use 2 pans so the bread won't overflow.

BREAD MACHINE VERSION

1. To proof the yeast, heat the water and milk to between 105°F-115°F. Add to the bread machine bowl fitted with the paddle. Add the yeast and sugar. Set aside for 5 minutes.
2. While the yeast is proofing, mix the dry ingredients in a separate mixing bowl: flour blend, xanthan gum, salt, and ginger.
3. Once the yeast mixture is foamy, add the liquid ingredients to the bread machine bowl: eggs, vinegar, oil, and honey or agave.
4. Carefully add flour mixture to the bread machine, one cup at a time, so that the flour mixture does not spill.
5. Turn machine on and select appropriate setting for a 2 pound loaf.
6. While dough is mixing, use a rubber spatula to scrape flour from the inside corners. Once the machine is done mixing, you can remove the paddle immediately and then smooth the top with a spatula. This way, the paddle is not stuck in the bread.
7. After bread is done, remove pan from machine and then remove bread from pan. Place on a wire rack. Carefully remove paddle, if still in the loaf (review manufacturer's instructions). Cool bread for at least 15 minutes before cutting. After 1 day, keep refrigerated.

STAND MIXER VARIATION

1. Place warm water and milk (see step 1 above) in a glass measuring cup or bowl. Add yeast and sugar and allow to proof for 5 minutes.
2. Add dry ingredients to the bowl of a stand mixer. Blend with a whisk to incorporate. When yeast is proofed, proceed to the next step.
3. In a small bowl, mix eggs, vinegar, oil, and honey or agave. Add this to the mixer and mix on low until blended.
4. Add the yeast mixture and mix to combine. Raise speed to medium and beat for 2-3 minutes until glossy. It should look like cake batter, not traditional bread dough.
5. With a greased spoon or spatula, fill 1 or 2 greased loaf pans no more than 2/3 full (see Chef Tips to left). Let dough rise for 50-60 minutes in a warm place until almost doubled in size.
6. Bake at 350°F for about 30-40 minutes or until brown on top. Allow bread to cool at least 15 minutes before cutting. After 1 day, keep refrigerated.

Everyday White Bread with Quick Rising Yeast

3¼ cups *Amy's Gluten-Free Flour Blend*
2 teaspoons xanthan gum
1 teaspoon sea or kosher salt
2¼ teaspoons quick rising yeast (1 packet)
⅛ teaspoon ground ginger (optional)

1 cup warm water (see note)
½ cup warm milk or milk substitute, plain and unsweetened (you can use all water instead of milk)

2 large eggs, beaten, at room temperature
1 teaspoon apple cider vinegar or white vinegar
1½ tablespoons olive oil or vegetable oil like safflower
1 tablespoon honey or agave nectar

Note: The liquid does not need to be hot for the quick rising yeast unless otherwise stated in manufacturer's directions.

Chef Tip

Measure the oil first and then the honey or agave so it does not stick to the measuring spoon.

BREAD MACHINE VERSION

1. Mix flour, xanthan gum, salt, yeast, and ginger in a medium bowl. Set aside.
2. Add warm water, milk, vinegar, oil, honey or agave, and eggs to the bread machine bowl fitted with the paddle.
3. Carefully add flour mixture to the bread machine, one cup at a time, so that the flour mixture does not spill.
4. Turn bread machine on. Use the Fast, Rapid, or Quick Bake setting for the quick rising yeast, about 60 minutes.
5. While dough is mixing, use a rubber spatula to scrape flour from the inside corners. Once the machine is done mixing, you can remove the paddle immediately and then smooth the top with a spatula. This way, the paddle is not stuck in the bread.
6. After bread is done, remove pan from machine and then remove bread from pan. Place on a wire rack. Carefully remove paddle, if still in the loaf (review manufacturer's instructions). Cool bread for at least 15 minutes before cutting. After 1 day, keep refrigerated.

STAND MIXER VARIATION

1. Add dry ingredients to the bowl of a stand mixer. Blend with a whisk to incorporate ingredients.
2. Mix eggs, vinegar, oil, and honey or agave in a small bowl. Set aside.
3. Combine milk and water; heat to 120°F-130°F.
4. Turn mixer on low and add both the milk/water and egg mixtures until blended. Raise speed to medium and beat for 2-3 minutes until glossy. It should look like cake batter, not traditional bread dough.
5. With a greased spoon or spatula, place in 1 or 2 greased loaf pans no more than ⅔ full (see Chef Tips on opposite page). Let dough rise for 20-25 minutes in a warm place.
6. Bake at 350°F for about 30-40 minutes or until brown on top. Allow bread to cool at least 15 minutes before cutting. After 1 day, keep refrigerated.

Flavor Variation

Chef Tips

When you are craving something a bit more brown and less white, this is the recipe for you. At the end of the day, make sure you have 3¼ cups total of "flour." It can be any combination of flour, gluten-free oats, or even flax seed. I have played with many different combinations and the results are always delicious.

Hopefully once you have made bread a few times, you won't need to look at the instructions; just the ingredients.

You only need to add the teaspoon of sugar to proof the regular or active yeast. Quick or rapid rise yeast is mixed with the dry ingredients; the extra teaspoon of sugar is not necessary.

Using molasses instead of honey or agave will produce a darker bread.

WHOLE GRAIN BREAD

Follow directions for *Everyday White Bread* (see prior page) but use the following ingredients.

2	cups *Amy's Gluten-Free Flour Blend*
½	cup sorghum flour
½	cup teff or buckwheat flour (make sure either flour is certified gluten-free if you are intolerant to gluten)
2	tablespoons gluten-free quick oats (or use regular gluten-free oats and chop them in a food processor)
2	tablespoons ground flax seed
2	teaspoons xanthan gum
1-1½	teaspoons sea or kosher salt (more or less depending upon your taste; less if you have regular salt)
⅛	teaspoon ground ginger (optional)
2¼	teaspoons regular or quick rising yeast (1 packet)
1	cup water (if using the optional ingredients below, add 1 extra tablespoon water)
½	cup milk (you can use all water instead of milk)
1	teaspoon sugar (for regular yeast)
1	teaspoon apple cider vinegar or white vinegar
1½	tablespoons olive oil or vegetable oil like safflower
1	tablespoon honey, agave nectar, or molasses
2	large eggs, beaten, at room temperature

OPTIONAL INGREDIENTS:

2	tablespoons each (up to 4 tablespoons total) unsalted sunflower seeds, pumpkin seeds, uncooked quinoa, or millet

Optional topping: 1 tablespoon gluten-free quick oats

Using teff or buckwheat flour creates a darker bread

Whole grain bread made with lighter flours, flax, and oats

Reuben sandwich made with "rye" bread

Tuna Melt

Everyday White Bread

Cinnamon Raisin Bread

Flavor Variation

"RYE"

2¼ cups *Amy's Gluten-Free Flour Blend*

½ cup gluten-free buckwheat or teff flour (for a lighter "rye," substitute the buckwheat or teff flour with *Amy's Gluten-Free Flour Blend*)

½ cup sorghum flour

2 tablespoons caraway seeds

1 tablespoon brown sugar or natural dark cane sugar (this replaces honey or agave)

2 teaspoons xanthan gum

1-1½ teaspoons sea or kosher salt

⅛ teaspoon ground ginger (optional)

2¼ teaspoons regular or quick rising yeast (1 packet)

1 cup water

½ cup milk or milk substitute, plain and unsweetened (you can use all water instead of milk)

1 teaspoon sugar (for regular yeast)

1 teaspoon apple cider vinegar or white vinegar

2 tablespoons olive oil or vegetable oil like safflower

2 large eggs, beaten, at room temperature

Growing up in New York, I always loved deli sandwiches but stopped eating them after going gluten-free. One day, I had a craving for a reuben so I adjusted my bread recipe to create this.

Once the bread was cool, I cut it into slices, buttered both outside pieces of the bread, and proceeded to make my sandwich with corned beef, swiss cheese, sauerkraut, and my own Russian dressing. I placed this in my panini maker (you can always use a non-stick pan over medium heat) and cooked it until the cheese was melted and the bread was golden brown. It really brought me back!

Follow directions for *Everyday White Bread* (see Index) but use the following ingredients.

For a darker "rye," use molasses instead of brown sugar.

Flavor Variation

CINNAMON RAISIN

This loaf is a nice treat for breakfast or a snack. Try it with butter, almond butter, or honey.

Follow directions for *Everyday White Bread* (see Index) but use the following ingredients..

Bread Machine: Add 1 teaspoon of ground cinnamon to the dry ingredients. After the dough has been mixing for about 3 minutes, add 1 cup of raisins. Most bread machines beep when it's time to add extra ingredients like dried fruit. Proceed with recipe.

Stand Mixer: Add 1 teaspoon of ground cinnamon to the dry ingredients. Once the dough has finished mixing, add 1 cup of raisins. Mix the dough for 20 seconds or until raisins are incorporated. Proceed with recipe.

Chef Tip

You can use Cinnamon Raisin bread to make a delicious *French toast* (see Index for recipe).

Quick Baguette

SIMPLE BAGUETTE

1½ **cups Amy's Gluten-Free Flour Blend (see note)**
2 **tablespoons almond flour**
1 **teaspoon baking powder**
¼ **teaspoon baking soda**
½ **teaspoon sea or kosher salt**
1 **teaspoon xanthan gum**

1 **large egg, beaten**
½ **cup plain yogurt (thicker yogurt is best, like European or Greek; in a pinch, use what you have)**
½ **cup sparkling water (I found mineral water gives the best results)**
2 **tablespoons olive or vegetable oil**

Note: If you want a whiter baguette, use 1 cup of the blend and ¼ each white rice flour and potato starch

Adapted from a recipe by Jacqueline Mallorca

Jacqueline Mallorca really is the gluten-free guru. I used one of her recipes to come up with this version of a quick and easy, yeast-free baguette. I sometimes bring this to a restaurant since we can't eat the regular bread. It's particularly good with olive oil and balsamic vinegar. I also use this baguette recipe to make what I call "fresh bruschetta." Instead of toasting the bread, I just cut it in half, spread it with pesto, and top with fresh veggies or burrata (Italian cheese similar to fresh mozzarella but creamier and tangy).

Makes 3 medium 10" baguettes

1. Preheat oven to 425°F and prepare pan. In order to make baguettes you need a baguette pan; otherwise the bread will not hold its shape. Place 1 piece of parchment perpendicular on top of indentations to cover the pan.
2. Mix dry ingredients (first 6 ingredients) in a large bowl.
3. Mix liquid ingredients (egg, yogurt, water, and oil) in a small or medium bowl and add to the dry ingredients. Mix together. Mix quickly for a few seconds to help the mixture gel.
4. Place tangerine-sized pieces of the dough on the pan to make 3 baguettes. Using a spatula, spread to form 3 pieces, being careful not to press too much so that the air bubbles do not pop.
5. Bake for 18 minutes. Baguettes should be brown.
6. Slide out of the pan, without the paper, and place bread directly on the oven rack. This will help make the outside crisp. Cook another 8-10 minutes. Baguette should sound hollow when tapped.

Flavor Variation

GRAINY BAGUETTE

Follow the instructions above except use ¾ cup of *Amy's Gluten-Free Flour Blend* and ¼ cup each of amaranth, sorghum, and quinoa flours (or some combination of those). Add 2 tablespoons ground flax seeds plus 2 tablespoons each of poppy and sunflower seeds.

If you want to put seeds on top, brush the baguettes with an egg wash (1 egg beaten with 1 teaspoon of milk) before placing them in the oven. Top with seeds and bake as directed above.

Soft Pizza Dough

2   large eggs, lightly beaten
3   tablespoons olive oil
1   teaspoon apple cider
     or white vinegar
1   tablespoon honey or agave nectar

1½   cups *Amy's Gluten-Free Flour Blend*
¼   cup white rice flour
¼   cup cornstarch
½   cup sorghum flour
2¼   teaspoons quick rising
     yeast (1 packet)
2   teaspoons xanthan gum
1   teaspoon sea or kosher salt
1   tablespoon white sugar

¾   cup hot water (heated
     to 120°F-130°F)

Notes: You can use 2½ cups of *Amy's Gluten-Free Flour Blend* and omit the white rice flour, cornstarch, and sorghum flour. The various flours are used to make the dough more white and less yellow. The millet flour in the flour blend gives it a yellow color.

If you use regular yeast, use warm water (105°F-115°F). Let dough rise for 45 minutes in step 8.

There are two things that are necessary for really good gluten-free pizza; par-baking the crust and a hot oven. I proved it by serving this pizza to a group of 6 and 7 year old (non gluten-free) boys at my son's 7th birthday party. I knew it was a success when their plates were empty.

The recipe might seem long, but I put in a lot of details. Make it a few times, and it won't seem hard at all. This recipe makes a fluffy, soft crust. If you like a thinner crust, divide the dough into two crusts rather than one. There is also a crispy, egg-less version on the next page. I have made it successfully by using only 2½ cups of my flour blend without the other flours or starch (see Note).

Makes 2 -12" pizzas

1. Place 1 or 2 pizza stones in the oven depending upon how many pizzas you are making. If you don't have a pizza stone, place parchment paper on a baking sheet.

2. Heat the oven to 200°F to get the stone and oven warm. Turn the oven off after 5 minutes.

3. Mix the eggs, olive oil, honey, and vinegar in a small bowl and set aside.

4. Add the dry ingredients to a bowl of a stand mixer fitted with the paddle (not the dough hook). Using a whisk, mix the dry ingredients. You can also mix on low with the paddle attachment.

5. Once you have all of your ingredients ready, turn the stand mixer on and add the egg and liquid mixture to the dry ingredients and mix for 10 seconds. Add the water. Raise the speed to medium and mix for 2-3 minutes. The dough will be sticky/tacky and will spread to the side of the bowl. It will look more like cake batter.

6. Cut a piece of parchment paper slightly smaller than the pizza stone or about 14" wide if you are using a tray. Place the parchment on a pizza peel or back of a baking tray, and lightly brush the paper with olive oil.

7. With a greased spatula or scooper, transfer pizza dough onto the middle of the paper. With greased hands, gently pat the pizza dough into a 12"-13" circle (or to the size of your pizza stone). If the dough is very sticky, add a little gluten-free flour blend on top to make it easier to handle. Once spread, make a crust or raised edge on the pizza by folding the edges over slightly toward the center. If you are going to flip the pizza after par-cooking, do not make a raised edge.

8. Slide the dough with the paper onto the stone in the oven. If you aren't using a stone, keep the dough on the baking sheet. Leave for 15-20 minutes to rise and then remove from oven by sliding the dough and paper back onto the peel or by removing the tray. Keep the stone in the oven.

9. Do not remove parchment paper from the dough. Heat the oven to 450°F for at least 20 minutes. Slide crust onto the stone and bake for 5-7 minutes or until crust is just starting to get light brown on the edges. If you don't have a stone, keep the crust on a baking sheet.

10. Remove the crust from the oven and cool briefly. Remove parchment paper. Optionally, for a crisper bottom, flip the crust over (see photo on opposite page).

11. Add sauce and toppings. Cook for about 7 minutes or until the crust is brown and the cheese is melted. Cool 3-5 minutes.

12. Use a pizza cutter or kitchen scissors to cut into pieces.

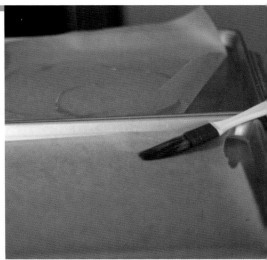

Crispy Pizza Dough

2½   cups *Amy's Gluten-Free Flour Blend*
½   cup sorghum flour
4½   teaspoons regular yeast (2 packets)
1   tablespoon xanthan gum
1   teaspoon sea or kosher salt

1⅓   cups hot water (between
     120°F -130°F)
1   teaspoon apple cider
     or white vinegar
2   tablespoons olive oil
1   tablespoon honey or agave nectar

OPTIONAL INGREDIENTS:
Olive oil
2   teaspoons cornmeal or corn
     flour (do not use polenta)

Chef Tip

There are two things that are necessary for really good gluten-free pizza; par-baking the crust and a hot oven.

I have been making gluten-free pizza for a number of years and I have finally found something that is almost as easy as "the old days," when I used to make pizza all of the time. This recipe is a combination of my white bread with a few changes, based on a recipe by Beth Hillson. The addition of the extra yeast and xanthan does make a difference. Make this a few times, and I bet you will find it easier each time. Homemade pizza is back!

Makes 2 -12" pizzas
Recipe can be halved to make a single pizza

1. Place 1 or 2 pizza stones in the oven. If you don't have a stone, you can use a baking sheet(s) but don't place them in the oven yet. Preheat oven to 450°F for at least 15 minutes before you are ready to bake the pizzas.
2. Add the dry ingredients (flours, yeast, xanthan gum, and salt) to the bowl of a stand mixer fitted with the paddle (not the dough hook). Using a whisk, mix the dry ingredients in the bowl to make sure the ingredients are well blended or blend with the paddle attachment.
3. Turn the stand mixer on low and add the hot water, vinegar, oil, and honey or agave. Mix for 30 seconds. Raise speed to medium and mix for 2-3 minutes. The dough will be sticky/tacky but will

almost be a ball (it is different from the Soft Pizza Crust recipe on the prior page).

4. Cut 2 pieces of parchment paper that are slightly smaller than the pizza stone or about 14" wide if you are using a tray. Place the parchment on top of a pizza peel or the bottom of a thin baking sheet turned upside down (this will act as the peel and help to slide the pizza onto the stone). Optionally brush the the paper with olive oil (I have made it both ways and like both versions). Optionally sprinkle about 1 teaspoon of cornmeal over the paper. This helps to give it that traditional pizza texture but is not necessary.

5. Decide how many pizzas you are making (2 large, 4 medium, or 6-8 personal). With a greased scooper or with greased hands, divide dough onto prepared sheets in small piles.
Note: If the dough feels very sticky, sprinkle 1 tablespoon of the gluten-free flour blend on top of the dough and pat it down.

6. Place a generous amount of oil on at least one hand. Working with one piece of dough at a time, pat into a circle. Pizza should be about ¼" thick. Fold the edges toward the center to make a crust. Prick all over with a fork to prevent uneven rising and bubbles.

7. Open oven. Carefully slide crust and parchment paper off of the pizza peel and onto the pizza stone. Bake crusts for 6-8 minutes or until just getting browned on the edges and on top. It should be a little puffy. Remove the crust from the oven, remove parchment, and place crust on a wire rack(s) to cool. See note below if you want to bake the crust later.

8. When you are ready to bake the pizza, make sure the oven has been heated to 450°F for at least 20 minutes with the pizza stone inside. If you don't have a stone, you can place the crust directly on the rack or use a baking sheet (perforated is best). Place pizza crusts either on a pizza paddle or pan. Add a thin layer of sauce, cheese, and toppings to the crust. Don't add too many toppings or the pizza will not be crisp.

9. Place pizza in oven and cook for about 12-15 minutes or until the crust is brown and the cheese is melted. Cool 3-5 minutes.

10. Use a pizza cutter or kitchen scissors to cut into pieces.

Note: If you want to finish cooking the pizza later, bake the crust as directed in step 7. Once it is cooled, wrap tightly in plastic. You can keep refrigerated and use within 48 hours or place in the freezer for up to 3 months. If it's been frozen, thaw for 5 minutes before using. Follow directions from step 8.

Pizza Sauce

1 15-ounce can tomato sauce
1 tablespoon olive oil
½ teaspoon sea or kosher salt
1 teaspoon Italian seasonings
   (see note), crumbled
   between your fingers

Note: If you don't have Italian seasonings, use ¼ teaspoon each garlic powder and thyme, and ½ teaspoon of oregano.

This is a technique I learned in Italy. I can't get over how simple this is yet how wonderful the flavor. Resist buying the pre-made sauce and try this one. The recipe is based on one from Wendy Holloway of Flavor of Italy. She runs a wonderful cooking school and bed and breakfast just outside of Rome, Italy.

Makes 2 cups

Mix ingredients in a bowl at least 15 minutes before using.

Kalamata olive, sun-dried tomato, and feta focaccia

Chef Tip

After you have placed the focaccia dough in the pan, spread generously with olive oil. Take your fingers and make indentations into the dough to give it that "focaccia" feel. It also helps to prevent bubbles and uneven rising.

Rosemary and sea salt focaccia

Bagels

2¼ teaspoons regular yeast (1 packet)
1 teaspoon sugar for proofing yeast
¾ cup warm water, heated
to 105°F-115°F

1½ cups + 2 tablespoons *Amy's
Gluten-Free Flour Blend*
½ cup white rice flour
¼ cup cornstarch
¼ cup sorghum flour
2 teaspoons xanthan gum
1 teaspoon sea or kosher salt
1½ tablespoons sugar plus 1
tablespoon for the boiling water

2 large eggs, at room temperature
½ teaspoon apple cider
or white vinegar
3 tablespoons olive oil
1 tablespoon honey or agave nectar

Olive or vegetable oil for rolling

OPTIONAL INGREDIENTS:
**Polenta or coarse cornmeal for dusting
the pan (for baking, not rising)**

**Egg wash: 1 teaspoon of water
plus 1 egg white, beaten**

**Sesame seeds, poppy seeds,
or coarse salt for topping**

I remember when my daughter first went gluten-free; the bagel options were less than stellar. This recipe was one of the first ones I mastered. It does involve 4 steps: making the dough, proofing, boiling, and baking. When you have the time, give it a try. The overall opinion is that these are worth it. This is one of the recipes in which I proof the yeast, even if it's quick rising. I think it gives it good flavor.

Makes 8 medium or 12 small bagels

1. Heat the oven to 200°F to get the oven warm. Turn the oven off after 5 minutes.
2. Prepare 2 baking sheets with parchment paper or silicone baking mats.
3. Place 1 teaspoon of sugar and the yeast in a glass measuring cup and add warm water. Mix and let it sit for 5 minutes until it's foamy. Set aside.
4. Mix the eggs in a small bowl. Add the vinegar, olive oil, and honey or agave nectar. Mix together with a fork or whisk. Set aside.
5. Add the dry ingredients to a bowl of a stand mixer fitted with the paddle (not the dough hook). Using a whisk, mix the dry ingredients in the bowl or mix with the paddle.
6. Turn the stand mixer on, and add the egg mixture to the dry ingredients, and give it a few twirls. Add the yeast mixture. Raise speed to medium and mix for 2-3 minutes. You want the dough to look like stiff cake batter. It should spread to the sides of the bowl of the mixer and will be very sticky.
7. Using a greased scoop or spatula, place about a ¼ cup ball of dough onto the baking sheets, leaving 2" between each bagel. Place oil on your hands and shape each piece into a bagel shape; round but slightly oblong and flat. Do not make the hole yet. Make sure the bagels are not stuck to the pan; otherwise it might be hard to remove them for the boiling step.
8. Place baking sheets in the warm oven. Let dough rise for 1 hour. Remove the trays from the oven.
9. About 15 minutes before the dough finishes rising, bring a large pot of water to a boil. Add 1 tablespoon of sugar. This helps to coat the outside of the bagels and make it a bit browner.
10. After the bagels have risen and have been removed from the oven, preheat oven to 400°F.
11. With a greased finger, poke a hole in center of each bagel. Rotate your finger around to make the hole a little bigger.

12. Bagels do not have to be boiled before baking but it is suggested. Working in small batches of 2-3 bagels at a time, carefully place bagels, top side down, in the boiling water for 25 seconds. You might want to use a flat spatula to transfer them to the water. If you want to add cornmeal to the bottom of the baking sheets, work quickly and sprinkle the cornmeal on the baking sheet in the empty spot while the bagels are boiling. Turn the bagels over using a slotted spoon and boil for another 20-25 seconds. Remove with a slotted spoon and place back on the prepared baking sheets. If using toppings, brush with egg wash and then add toppings. The egg wash helps to adhere the seed to the bagel.

13. Bake for 20-24 minutes, rotating trays once, until golden brown.

14. After 3-5 minutes, place on wire racks to cool. Refrigerate leftovers. Once cool, bagels can be frozen for up to 4 months in an airtight bag.

Cornbread

1   **cup cornmeal (fine, not coarse)**
¾   **cup Amy's Gluten-Free Flour Blend or garbanzo bean flour**
2-4 **tablespoons sugar (use less if you do not like sweet cornbread)**
2   **teaspoons baking powder**
½   **teaspoon xanthan gum**
½   **teaspoon sea or kosher salt**

1   **large egg, lightly beaten**
1   **cup milk or milk substitute (plain and unsweetened)**
¼   **cup vegetable oil or melted butter**

OPTIONAL INGREDIENTS:
½   **cup frozen corn, slightly thawed, or fresh corn, cut from the cob**
½   **cup shredded cheddar**
¼   **cup diced mild green chiles**

Cornbread can be served at practically any meal. It's delicious with butter or jam or as a side with chili or soup. This recipe is easy to make casein-free by using a milk substitute and oil instead of butter.

Makes 1- 9" × 9" or 8" × 8" pan

1. Preheat the oven to 400°F. Grease a 9" × 9" or 8" × 8" square pan.
2. In a large bowl, combine the dry ingredients (first 6 ingredients).
3. In a medium bowl, combine the egg, milk, and oil or butter and whisk to combine.
4. Pour the wet ingredients into the dry ingredients and stir. Add the optional ingredients if you are using. Stir for about 20-30 seconds. Pour the batter into the prepared pan.
5. Bake for 15-18 minutes until the cornbread begins to pull away from the sides of the pan, is golden in color, and springs back to the touch. If you overcook, it will be dry.
6. Cool in pan for 10 minutes before cutting.
7. Once cool, cornbread can be stored in the pan or removed to a storage dish or resealable plastic bag. Keep refrigerated.

Note: To make into muffins, prepare a 12-cup muffin tin by either greasing or placing liners inside. Fill cups with batter about ⅔ full. Bake at 400°F for 14-16 minutes or until the muffin springs back when touched.

Drop Biscuits

⅓ cup unsalted butter (use shortening for dairy-free)

DRY INGREDIENTS

1½ cups white rice flour
½ cup potato starch
1-2 tablespoons white sugar (use less if you don't like a sweet biscuit)
2 teaspoons baking powder
1 teaspoon sea or kosher salt
1 teaspoon xanthan gum

LIQUID INGREDIENTS

3 large eggs
⅔ cup whole milk or milk substitute, plain and unsweetened
1 teaspoon apple cider or white vinegar

Makes 12-16 Biscuits

1. Place butter or shortening in the freezer for 5 minutes to chill while you measure the other ingredients.
2. Preheat oven to 400°F. Prepare a baking sheet with parchment paper or a silicone baking mat.
3. Place dry ingredients in the bowl of a food processor and pulse to mix. If you don't have a processor, place the dry ingredients in a medium bowl and mix with a whisk to combine.
4. In another small bowl, mix the liquid ingredients. Set aside.
5. Add cold butter or shortening to the processor. Pulse for 10-20 seconds or until butter or shortening is chopped. The mixture should look like grated Parmesan cheese. If you don't have a food processor, use a pastry blender to blend the butter or shortening with the flour mixture, or use two knifes to "cut" the butter or shortening into the flour mixture.
6. Remove butter (or shortening) and flour mixture and add to a medium sized bowl. Add liquid ingredients and mix until a dough forms.
7. Using a large spoon, drop the dough onto the prepared pan to make 12-16 biscuits.
8. Bake for 15 minutes or until golden brown.

Variations

SWEET BISCUITS FOR DESSERTS

Use this biscuit recipe for strawberry shortcakes or fruit cobbler. Use ¼ cup of white sugar instead of 1-2 tablespoons. Sprinkle biscuits with 2 teaspoons of white sugar before baking.

CHEDDAR BISCUITS

You can serve cheddar biscuits with chili or as an appetizer with sliced ham or turkey inside. Add ¼ teaspoon of dry mustard to the dry ingredients. Add ¾ cup of shredded cheddar cheese (mild or sharp) in step 6.

Cheddar Crisps

5 tablespoons unsalted cold butter

¼ pound (about 1 cup packed) shredded extra-sharp cheddar cheese (or use a combo of cheeses)

¾ cup *Amy's Gluten-Free Flour Blend* plus extra for shaping

¼ teaspoon xanthan gum

2 tablespoons cornmeal

1 large egg

½ teaspoon kosher or flaky sea salt

OPTIONAL INGREDIENTS:

40 Pumpkin seeds

Chef Tip

These cheddar crisps can be shaped into "fingers" for a fun snack. Add a pumpkin seed at the tip for a fingernail.

We first made these around Halloween as Witch's Fingers. I had adapted a regular recipe to make it gluten-free. It will be sticky but don't worry because that is normal. Just follow the directions. The biggest problem I found with this recipe was trying to stop myself from eating the whole batch!

Adapted from a recipe from Sunset Magazine

Makes about thirty-six 5" strips

1. In a food processor, mix together butter, cheese, ¾ cup of the flour blend, xanthan gum, and cornmeal until the mixture has the texture of wet sand. If you don't have a food processor, place the ingredients in a medium bowl. Use two knifes to "cut" the butter and cheese into the other ingredients. Set aside.

2. Place egg in a large bowl and beat. Add cheese and flour mixture to the egg. Stir with with a fork until dough holds together. It will be very sticky.

3. Using your hands and the extra flour, pat dough into a disc. Cut a piece of plastic wrap that is about 22" long. Wrap the disc in the plastic and freeze 15 minutes, or refrigerate for at least 30 minutes and up to 3 days.

4. Remove from fridge and let sit on the counter for a few minutes. Position disc on plastic wrap so when the plastic wrap is folded in half, the disc is in the middle. Roll the dough between the pieces of plastic into a rectangle about 8" × 10" long (the size of a regular piece of paper). Return to freezer or fridge for 15 minutes. Prepare two baking sheets with either silicone baking mats or parchment paper.

5. Preheat oven to 350°F. Peel off half of the plastic. Using a paring knife, cut dough in half down the longer side. Cut dough in the other direction to make ¾"–1" strips.

6. Carefully place on the baking sheets about ½" apart. Sprinkle with salt. To make fingers, score each piece with a knife and press a pumpkin seed into one end.

7. Bake the strips until they are an even light brown, about 15 minutes, rotating the pans once. Let cool on pans for 5 minutes then transfer to a wire rack to finish cooling.

Contents

Desserts and Treats

Baking is an easy way to create a warm kitchen. Gluten-free desserts have come a long way since 2006 when I started cooking and baking. Many of these recipes contained gluten containing flours which I have since converted (I have had the carrot cake recipe for 20 years!). Others were created after playing with ingredients, like the fruit crisp. The bottom line is after serving these dishes to family, friends, and cooking class participants, everyone says the same thing, "This is gluten-free? I would have never known!"

The recipes range from the very basic to just a little complicated. None of them are hard in my opinion. The bottom line is that these desserts taste great and have wonderful texture. Really, you can make a pie crust!

I don't claim to have created every recipe in this section but, if I use someone else's, I give them credit and have changed at least 1-2 ingredients as well as the directions. In baking, you have to start somewhere. I hope you enjoy this chapter. In case it's been a while, let them eat cake!

See the *Stocking the Pantry* and *Common Substitutions* chapters for more information on gluten-free ingredients, substitutions, and instructions for making *Amy's Gluten-Free Flour Blend*. Always check ingredients to make sure they are gluten-free.

See the baking tips for muffins in the beginning of the *Breakfast and Brunch* chapter (see Index).

Chef Tips

See the baking tips for muffins in the beginning of the *Breakfast and Brunch* chapter (see Index). Many of these apply to making desserts as well.

You can substitute fine sea salt for kosher salt. If you use table salt, use 25% (one fourth) less.

Desserts

DAIRY-FREE SUBSTITUTIONS FOR DESSERTS

Many traditional dessert recipes use regular milk and butter which some people cannot have. I refer to the substitutions as dairy-free but really, these are casein-free. Casein is the protein found in milk that many people cannot tolerate. Here are common substitutions.

- Vegetable shortening, like Spectrum™, works really well in cakes and for frosting. I like the organic variety that is not hydrogenated. Keep it at room temperature. When I make cakes I usually beat the butter or shortening with the sugar to get the batter fluffy. The shortening should be slightly warm to make this process easier.

- Coconut oil works really well in madeleines. It's not bad in cake but can make it a bit greasy due to its low melting point. Make sure to heat it first so it is easy to measure, then cool slightly.

- Most milk substitutes (soy, rice, coconut, almond, etc.) are a good replacement for milk. You can also add vinegar to make "buttermilk" for any of the recipes. Buttermilk can be made with any type of milk substitute (see *Chef Tips* on the following page).

- For sour cream, you can substitute a soy based "sour cream," dairy-free yogurt, or make your own "sour cream". To make your own substitute, measure ⅞ cup (1 cup less 2 tablespoons) of "buttermilk" and then add 2 tablespoons of fat to measure 1 cup. Examples of fat are vegetable oil, melted coconut oil, or melted shortening.

EGG-FREE SUBSTITUTIONS FOR DESSERTS

If you need to substitute eggs as well, be sure to test the substitution first. It's tricky to substitute gluten, dairy, and eggs in one recipe. Here are the substitutions which I find work well for 2 large eggs:

- ¼ cup applesauce mixed with 2 teaspoons baking powder +1 tablespoon vegetable oil +1 tablespoon water.

- 5 tablespoons water + 1 tablespoon oil + 1 tablespoon ground flaxseed + 2 teaspoons baking powder (mix in a small bowl and wait 5-10 minutes). If you use this substitution for vanilla cake, you will see the flax flecks. Try the one above.

- Store-bought egg substitute (follow directions for 3 eggs to substitute 2 large eggs).

How To Make It...
Easy as 1, 2, 3

BASIC CAKE

1 Mix dry ingredients in a bowl.

2 Cream together butter or shortening and sugar. Add eggs one at a time.

3 Add milk and dry ingredients in 2-3 additions. Portion and bake.

Chef Tips: Making Cakes

- To make your own buttermilk, place 1 tablespoon of white vinegar or lemon juice in a glass measuring cup. Add milk or milk substitute to fill 1 cup. Let sit for 5 minutes. This recipe can be scaled if you need more or less.

- Ginger is a natural preservative. Add ⅛ of a teaspoon to the dry ingredients to keep cakes and cupcakes fresh a few days more.

- When I baked regular cakes which called for cake flour, I would substitute ¼ cup of the regular flour with cornstarch to lighten it up. I do the same with my gluten-free cake recipes. If you can't have corn, use arrowroot.

- A cake will rise better if the ingredients are at room temperature. Bring eggs to room temperature quickly by placing them in hot water for 5 minutes.

- If you don't have a stand mixer, you will need an electric hand mixer with beaters (see left). You need this to incorporate the air into the butter and sugar as well as the eggs.

- When mixing the cake, make sure to scrape down the sides of the bowl so that the ingredients are all incorporated.

- Make sure to use cupcake liners for cupcakes and to dust greased pans with gluten-free flour for all cake pans.

- Cupcakes should only be filled about ⅔ or else they might overflow. The same goes for a cake pan.

- Most cupcake recipes can be made into cakes; reduce the oven temperature by 25°F and increase the cooking time by about 10-15 minutes.

- In gluten free baking, the tooth pick test doesn't work to check for doneness in cakes and cupcakes. Press the center of the cupcake or cake. When it springs back, it is done. If it leaves an indentation, it needs to bake another 1-2 minutes. Also, the cake should pull away from the side of the pan.

- A good time to check a cake for doneness is when you can smell it. Even if my timer has not gone off, if I smell the cake, I check it.

Vanilla cupcake
with buttercream
frosting

Photo by Gretchen Martini of Studio

❤ Chef Tip: Measuring Flour

When measuring flour, don't pack the flour into
the measuring cup. Scoop up about half into the
cup then use a scoop or another cup to place flour
on top. Once the flour is heaping, use a straight
edge like a knife, and level the top. If you pack
the flour in, you can use too much flour and then
your baked good will be dry.

Vanilla Cake or Cupcakes

This recipe takes a little more effort but is certainly well worth it!

Makes 18-24 cupcakes or two 8" cakes

2	cups *Amy's Gluten-Free Flour Blend*
¼	cup cornstarch
¾	teaspoon baking soda
½	teaspoon baking powder
½	teaspoon kosher salt
¾	teaspoon xanthan gum
⅛	teaspoon ground ginger (optional)
½	cup unsalted butter or vegetable shortening, softened, or vegetable oil
1¼	cups white sugar
2	large eggs, at room temperature
½	cup plain yogurt, sour cream or buttermilk (see Index), at room temperature
2	teaspoons vanilla extract

1. Preheat oven to 350°F. Line 2 standard-sized muffin pans with liners or grease generously or grease and "flour" two 8" cake pans.
2. In a medium bowl, mix the dry ingredients (first 7 ingredients) with a whisk until combined. Set aside.
3. Place butter, shortening or oil in the bowl of a stand mixer. If using vegetable oil, proceed to next step. Cream butter or shortening for 20-30 seconds.
4. With mixer on low, add sugar. Turn mixer to medium and cream for 3 minutes, scraping down the bowl once with a spatula.
5. Add eggs one at a time and mix until well combined, scraping down the bowl in between.
6. Mix the buttermilk and vanilla in a bowl. Alternating between the milk mixture and the flour mixture, add to the butter and sugar mixture in 3 additions. After everything has been added, scrape down the bowl. Mix on medium for 20 seconds.
7. Fill cupcake liners ⅔ full and bake about 18-20 minutes. Cupcakes are done when they are golden on top and they spring back after touching; the toothpick test doesn't always work.
8. Cool for 5 minutes and then remove from cupcake pan. Cool completely on wire racks. Store in the fridge.

Variations:

Coconut Cake: Add ½ cup shredded sweetened coconut at the end of step 6, after the milk and flour mixtures have been added. Frost with *Vanilla Buttercream Frosting* (see Index) and top with sweetened shredded coconut.

Lemon Cake: Use an extra 2 tablespoons of *Amy's Gluten-Free Flour Blend*. To the buttermilk, add ¼ cup fresh lemon juice. Add ¼ cup of lemon zest at the end of step 6, after the milk and flour mixtures have been added.

Easy Vanilla Cake or Cupcakes

1	tablespoon white vinegar or lemon juice
⅔	cup whole milk or milk substitute
1	cup *Amy's Gluten-Free Flour Blend*
¼	cup white rice flour
¼	cup cornstarch
½	teaspoon baking powder
¼	teaspoon kosher salt
½	teaspoon xanthan gum
⅛	teaspoon ground ginger
2	large eggs, at room temperature
2	teaspoons vanilla extract
¾	cup white sugar
½	cup melted unsalted butter or vegetable shortening

This is a favorite with my kids and friends. Most people can't believe it's gluten-free; always a good sign. I encourage you to try it rather than using a mix. In case you are wondering, I use the white rice flour to make it a little "whiter" and lighter. You could use all of the flour blend instead.

Makes 12 cupcakes or one 13" × 9" cake (this recipe does not double well; it's better to make it twice)

1. Preheat oven to 350°F. Line a 12-cup muffin pan with liners or grease a 13" × 9" pan.
2. Mix milk and vinegar in a glass measuring cup and set aside for at least 5 minutes.
3. In a medium bowl, mix the dry ingredients (next 7 ingredients) with a whisk or fork until combined. Set aside.
4. Whisk eggs and vanilla in large bowl until well blended. In a steady stream, pour sugar into eggs, whisking constantly. Gradually whisk in melted butter or shortening, then add milk and vinegar mixture.
5. Add dry ingredients in 3 additions using a whisk to combine. It's alright if a few streaks of flour should remain in between. After all of the flour is added, stir the batter briskly for 20 seconds.
6. Fill cupcake liners 2/3 full. Place cupcake pan on the middle rack, until cupcakes just begin to color and the cupcake springs back, 18-22 minutes. Cool pans on wire racks for 5 minutes then remove cupcakes from pans, place back on rack, and cool to room temperature before frosting, about 1 hour.
7. For cake, bake in greased 13" × 9" pan for about 30 minutes.

Note: Keep leftovers refrigerated after 1 day so that the cupcakes or cake stays fresher.

The makings of a Willy Wonka cake. The center is the chocolate river.

Dairy and Egg-Free Vanilla Cupcakes

1	cup milk substitute
1	tablespoon white vinegar or lemon juice
¼	cup applesauce
2	teaspoons baking powder
1	tablespoon vegetable oil
1	tablespoon water
2	cups *Amy's Gluten-Free Flour Blend*
1	cup white sugar
½	teaspoon kosher salt
1	teaspoon baking powder
1	teaspoon baking soda
1	teaspoon xanthan gum
¼	cup coconut oil or vegetable shortening, melted
2	teaspoons vanilla extract

While we were trying to rule out some food sensitivities, my daughter was on a gluten-free, dairy-free and egg-free diet for a while. Birthday parties were quite a challenge so I had to get good at an easy recipe I could whip up easily. This is the one.

Makes 18-24 cupcakes or one 13" × 9" cake

1. Preheat the oven to 350°F. Line two 12-cupcake pans with liners or grease a 13" × 9" pan.
2. Measure the milk substitute and add the vinegar or lemon juice; set aside.
3. Mix the applesauce, baking powder, oil and water in a small bowl (this is the egg substitute) and set aside.
4. In a large bowl, mix the flour, sugar, salt, baking powder, baking soda, and xanthan gum together.
5. Add the milk substitute mixture, egg substitute mixture, coconut or vegetable oil, and vanilla. Mix together until smooth.
6. Using a hinged scooper, portion batter into cups, filling 2/3 full. Bake about 15-18 minutes. Cupcakes will spring back when they are done. For cake, bake for about 27-30 minutes.
7. Cool pans on wire racks for 5 minutes then remove cupcakes from pans, place back on rack, and cool to room temperature before frosting, about 1 hour.

Note: Keep leftovers refrigerated after 1 day so that the cupcakes or cake stays fresher.

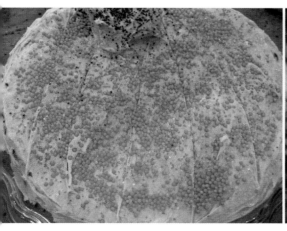

Dark Chocolate Cupcakes

½   cup unsalted butter, cut into 4 pieces, or vegetable shortening

2   ounces bittersweet chocolate

½   cup Dutch-processed cocoa
¾   cup *Amy's Gluten-Free Flour Blend*
¾   teaspoon baking powder
½   teaspoon baking soda
½   teaspoon kosher salt
¼   heaping teaspoon xanthan gum
⅛   teaspoon ground ginger (optional)

2   large eggs, at room temperature
¾   cup white sugar
1   teaspoon vanilla extract
½   cup sour cream or plain yogurt (full-fat is best)

For dairy-free, see *Dairy-Free Substitutions for Desserts* (see Index).

I served these cupcakes for my son's birthday one year. It was memorable because the non gluten-free boys not only ate the frosting, but devoured the cupcake as well. I did make two separate batches because this recipe does not double very well. However, I was able to reuse a lot of the equipment so it wasn't too difficult.

Makes 12 cupcakes

1. Preheat oven to 350°F. Line a 12-cup muffin pan with liners.
2. Melt butter or shortening and chocolate either in a metal or glass bowl over a pan of simmering water or in a microwave-safe bowl. Microwave in 30-40 second intervals, stirring in between, until melted. Set aside to cool but make sure it's still liquid.
3. Whisk dry ingredients (next 7 ingredients) in a bowl to combine. Set aside.
4. Whisk eggs in another medium bowl to combine. Add sugar and mix briskly for 2 minutes. Add vanilla and stir. Mix in sour cream or yogurt. Add chocolate and butter mixture.
5. Add flour mixture, and mix until it is all combined. Mix briskly for 20 seconds.
6. Divide batter evenly among muffin pan cups. Bake 16-20 minutes or until the top springs back when pushed in.
7. Cool for 5 minutes then remove from pan and place on a wire rack. Cool completely before frosting. Store cupcakes in the refrigerator.

"Brown" Velvet Natural Cupcakes

1   15-ounce undrained can whole beets (not pickled)

2¼   cups *Amy's Gluten-Free Flour Blend*
⅓   cup corn starch
1½   tablespoons cocoa powder
1   teaspoon baking soda
1   teaspoon baking powder
½   teaspoon kosher salt
½   teaspoon xanthan gum
⅛   teaspoon ground ginger

1¼   cups white sugar
½   cup butter or shortening, softened
2   large eggs, room temperature

½   cup sour cream
¼   cup milk or milk substitute
1   tablespoon vinegar
1   teaspoon vanilla extract

For dairy-free, see *Dairy-Free Substitutions for Desserts* (see Index)

I know many people who have children that cannot have red velvet cupcakes because of the food coloring. I decided to try to make these natural and gluten-free. The result is a pinkish-topped, light brown inside cupcake. After trying 6 different combinations, I realized my daughter mostly liked the taste and was not so unnerved with the fact that they weren't red inside. Sure, you can use natural food coloring but it's very expensive. These are almost red and super tasty. The magenta-colored batter is quite fun as well. Save some of the beet liquid to use for frosting to give it a pink tint. Read through the recipe first as there are a number of steps including cooking down the beet juice to make it extra red (really pink).

Makes 18-24 cupcakes

1. Carefully drain liquid from the beets and place the liquid in a small sauce pan. The juice can stain your clothes and counter so be careful. Simmer liquid until reduced by half. You want at least ¼ cup of reduced liquid. Cool slightly.
2. Place about ⅓-½ cup of the whole beets in a food processor with 1 or 2 teaspoons of water. Process until almost smooth, scraping down the sides. Add more water if necessary but slowly. Measure ¼ cup of the beet puree and ¼ cup of the concentrated beet juice and place in a small bowl. Set aside.
3. Preheat the oven to 350°F. Prepare two 12-cup cupcake pans with liners.
4. Mix the dry ingredients (next 8 ingredients) in a medium bowl with a whisk. Set aside.
5. Place the butter or shortening in the bowl of a stand mixer fitted with the paddle attachment (alternatively use a large bowl and an electric mixer). Mix butter or shortening for 30 seconds. Add sugar and beat for 2 minutes or until combined.
6. Add the eggs, one at a time. Beat until each is fully incorporated, scraping down the sides of the bowl.
7. In a glass measuring cup or bowl, mix together the buttermilk, ¼ cup beet juice, ¼ cup beet puree, vanilla and vinegar.
8. Add a third of the wet ingredients to the batter and mix on low. Add a third of the dry ingredients to the sugar and butter mixture and mix. Repeat 2 more times. Mix on medium for 10-15 seconds; this helps gel the xanthan gum.
9. Fill cupcake liners ⅔ full. Bake 18-22 minutes, rotating pans once (switching racks). Cupcakes are done when you press the center and it springs back. The toothpick test does not work.
10. Cool for 2 minutes in the pan then transfer to a wire rack to cool completely.

Banana Cupcakes

2 cups **Amy's Gluten-Free Flour Blend**
¼ cup cornstarch
¾ teaspoon baking soda
½ teaspoon baking powder
½ teaspoon kosher salt
½ heaping teaspoon xanthan gum
¼ teaspoon cinnamon (optional)
⅛ teaspoon ground ginger (optional)

½ cup buttermilk, at room temperature
1 cup ripe bananas, about 2-3

½ cup unsalted butter or shortening, softened, or vegetable oil
1¼ cups white sugar
2 large eggs, at room temperature
1 teaspoon vanilla extract

OPTIONAL INGREDIENTS:
½ cup chopped nuts (walnuts or pecans)
½ cup shredded unsweetened coconut

For dairy-free, see *Dairy-Free Substitutions for Desserts* (see Index)

Everyone always thinks to make banana bread or muffins when the bananas are ripe. Try these delicious cupcakes for a treat with Vanilla Buttercream Frosting *or* Best Cream Cheese Frosting *(see Index).*

Makes 18-24 cupcakes

1. Preheat oven to 350°F and prepare pans with cupcake liners.
2. In a medium bowl, mix the dry ingredients (first 8 ingredients) with a whisk or fork until combined. Set aside.
3. Prepare buttermilk (see Index, *Making Buttermilk*). Set aside.
4. Place bananas in a medium bowl and mash. Set aside.
5. Place butter, shortening, or oil in the bowl of a stand mixer. If using vegetable oil, proceed to next step. Cream butter or shortening for 45 seconds.
6. With mixer on low, add sugar. Turn mixer to medium and cream for 3 minutes, scraping down the bowl once with a spatula.
7. Add eggs, one at a time and mix until well combined.
8. Mix the banana, buttermilk and vanilla in a bowl. Alternating between the banana mixture and the flour mixture, add to the batter, in 3 additions. After everything has been added, scrape down the bowl. Add the nuts and coconut if using. Mix on medium for 20 seconds.
9. Fill cupcake liners ⅔ full and bake about 18-20 minutes. Cupcakes are done when they are golden on top and they spring back after touching; the toothpick test doesn't always work.
10. Cool for 5 minutes and then remove from cupcake pan. Cool completely on wire racks. Store in the fridge.

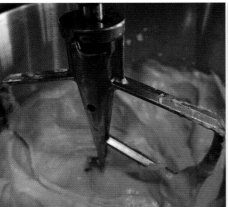

Carrot Cake

2¼ cups **Amy's Gluten-Free Flour Blend**
2 teaspoons baking powder
1½ teaspoons baking soda
¾ teaspoon xanthan gum
2 teaspoons cinnamon
1 teaspoon kosher salt
⅛ teaspoon ground ginger

4 large eggs, at room temperature
¾-1 cup white sugar
¾ cup brown sugar
¾ cup vegetable oil
½ cup unsweetened applesauce
3 cups grated carrot
½ cup chopped walnuts (optional)
½ cup raisins
½ cup shredded unsweetened coconut

I have been making this cake for 20 years (oh my; that makes me sound old!). I adapted it to gluten-free a few years ago with great success; as a bonus, it is naturally dairy-free as well. This dessert is always a big hit at parties.

Makes one 13"× 9" cake, two 8" round cakes or 18-24 cupcakes

1. Preheat oven to 350°F. Grease a 13" × 9" pan, 2-8" or 9" round pans, or line two 12-cup muffin tins with liners.
2. Mix dry ingredients (first 7 ingredients) in a medium bowl with a whisk. Set aside.
3. In a large bowl, mix the eggs first. Add sugars, oil, and applesauce. Use more sugar if you like a slightly sweeter cake. Fold in carrot, nuts, raisins and coconut.
4. Add the dry ingredients to the carrot and mix. Give the batter a few quick twirls.
5. Pour into pan(s) or fill cupcakes to ⅔ full and place in oven. Bake for 35-45 minutes for the large pan, 25-28 minutes for the round cake pans and 19-21 minutes for cupcakes. When you start to smell the cake, start testing. Bake until the cake pulls away from the sides of the pan and the cake springs back in the middle when touched.
6. Cool the cake in pan. If you made 2 cakes, cool for 5 minutes, then flip onto a wire rack to cool. If you made cupcakes, remove the cupcakes from the pan and cool on wire racks.
7. Once cake(s) are completely cool, top with either *Vanilla Buttercream Frosting* or *Best Cream Cheese Frosting* (see Index).

Chocolate Whoopie Pies

1	cup *Amy's Gluten-Free Flour Blend*
⅓	cup unsweetened cocoa powder
½	teaspoon baking soda
½	teaspoon xanthan gum
¼	teaspoon kosher salt
¼	cup unsalted butter or shortening, softened
½	cup white sugar
1	large egg
½	teaspoon vanilla extract
½	cup milk or milk substitute

Frosting/filling of choice like *Classic Marshmallow Filling* (see right), *Vanilla Buttercream*, *Whipped Cream* or *Peanut Butter Cream Cheese Frosting* (see Index for recipes)

Note: When making frosting as the filling, add extra milk so it's creamy and easy to spread.

Whoopie pies are quite popular on the East coast. These tasty little "pies" are usually made of a chocolate cake-like cookie and filled with a cream frosting. You won't need a whoopie pie pan; just a good baking sheet and some parchment or a silicone mat. If you've ever made cake, you can make these. And you'll be hard-pressed to be able to tell the difference between these and those made with regular flour. Just make sure to eat them within a day or two; otherwise freeze the pies and add the filling later.

Makes 6 medium or 10 small pies

1. Preheat oven to 350°F. Prepare 2 baking sheets by lining with parchment paper or silicone baking mats.
2. In a medium bowl, mix the dry ingredients (first 5 ingredients).
3. Place the butter or shortening and sugar in a large bowl. With an electric mixer, cream the butter and sugar on low. Increase speed until well combined. Add the egg and vanilla, and mix to combine. Add the milk, and beat until uniformly smooth, then add the flour mixture. Continue to beat until the batter becomes thicker and a bit more elastic.
4. Using a hinged scooper, pastry bag or two tablespoons, portion batter onto baking sheets, trying to keep a rounded shape. Make sure pies are uniform in shape and that you portion an even number of them so that you have a top and bottom. Using a rubber spatula, spread them just a bit to flatten so they are more like a cookie; otherwise when they bake they will be like a dome.
5. Place baking sheets in oven and bake for 8-10 minutes rotating once during baking. To test for doneness, press your finger into the center of the pie. When it springs back, it's done. If it leaves an indentation, continue to bake and test in 1-2 minute intervals.
6. Remove from the oven and keep on the tray for 7-10 minutes. Using a spatula, carefully transfer pies to a wire rack and cool completely.
7. Once the cookies are cool, arrange pies that are similar in shape next to each other. Place about 2 tablespoons of frosting on one side and spread evenly to the edges; use less if you made them smaller. Place the other pie on top and smooth out the frosting on the sides. Optionally, you can pipe through a pastry bag with a wide circle tip in a circular motion from the outside, piping in.

Note: I like my frosting a bit firm and not squishy so I keep them chilled until ready to serve. However, unless you use a cream cheese or whipped cream based frosting, you do not need to refrigerate.

Classic Marshmallow Filling

¾ cup softened vegetable shortening or unsalted butter (the shortening is more traditional)
1 cup marshmallow fluff or cream
¾-1 cup confectioners' sugar
1 teaspoon vanilla extract

VARIATION
For a chocolate peppermint flavor, use ½ teaspoon peppermint extract instead of the vanilla in the frosting

This is the classic marshmallow filling you will find in bakery-made pies. I adjusted it slightly to make the right amount for the Chocolate Whoopie Pie recipe.

1. Place the shortening or butter in a large bowl or a stand mixer fitted with the paddle attachment. Beat briefly to make sure it is soft; otherwise, it will not blend with the marshmallow. Add marshmallow cream and beat until well combined.
2. Add ¾ cup of the sugar and the extract. Mix until well blended. Taste. Add more sugar if necessary.
3. Mix on medium speed for about a minute or until fluffy.

These frostings are all naturally gluten-free and delicious. When you see how easy these frostings are, you will never want anything else. Enjoy!

Vanilla Buttercream Frosting

1 cup unsalted butter, room temperature
6-8 cups confectioners' sugar
2-4 tablespoons milk
1 teaspoon vanilla extract

Makes enough frosting for 24-30 cupcakes or 2 cakes. This recipe can be halved.

In the bowl of an electric mixer fitted with the paddle attachment, cream butter until smooth and creamy, 2-3 minutes. With mixer on low speed, add 6 cups sugar, milk, and vanilla; mix until light and fluffy. If necessary, gradually add remaining 2 cups sugar to reach desired consistency, thick enough to spread but not too thick.

VARIATION: CHOCOLATE FROSTING

Melt 1 cup semisweet chocolate chips either in the microwave in a bowl (30 second intervals until melted) or in a metal bowl, over a pan of simmering water. Set aside and let cool slightly. Follow recipe above but reduce butter to 1½ sticks and replace ¼ cup of confectioners' sugar with ¼ cup unsweetened cocoa powder. Once the sugar and cocoa have been added, beat in melted chocolate and proceed as directed. You may need to add more confectioners' sugar to reach proper consistency

Dairy-Free Creamy Frosting

1 cup vegetable shortening, softened
4-6 cups confectioners' sugar
1 teaspoon vanilla extract
2 tablespoons milk substitute

Makes enough frosting for about 24 cupcakes or one large cake. This recipe can be halved.

In a stand mixer fitted with a paddle, beat the shortening for 30 seconds. Add 4 cups of the sugar, the vanilla and milk substitute. Mix until blended and then increase speed to medium and beat for another 3 minutes until light and fluffy. Add more sugar if frosting is too thin.

Whipped Cream

Makes about 2 cups

1 cup heavy or whipping cream
1-2 tablespoons white sugar
½ teaspoon vanilla extract

Chill beaters and bowl before making. This helps the air incorporate into the cream.

Whip cream until there are soft peaks. Add sugar and vanilla; beat until cream holds firm peaks. Make sure not to overbeat or else you will make butter. Keep refrigerated.

Chef Tips: Frosting

If you don't have a stand mixer and you want to be able to make cakes and frosting, invest in a handheld mixer which does not take up a lot of space and costs much less.

When you are filling the pastry bag with frosting, place the bag in a 16-ounce or larger glass and fold the bag over the sides. You have much more control when filling the pastry bag. Close the bag up, twist and squeeze to pipe frosting.

The best combination is a cold cake and room temperature frosting. Chill the cake for at least 2 hours before frosting. If you have to make the frosting ahead, make sure it's softened before spreading. You can put the frosted cake in the fridge to firm up the frosting.

Most frosting (except cream cheese) does not need to be refrigerated. Bacterial growth in buttercream frosting is inhibited due to the high amount of fat.

Best Cream Cheese Frosting

½ cup unsalted butter, room temperature

6 ounces cream cheese, room temperature

4-6 cups confectioners' sugar, sifted

1 tablespoon milk

½ teaspoon vanilla extract

Makes enough frosting for about 24 cupcakes or one large cake. This recipe can be halved.

Beat butter and cream cheese with a mixer on medium-high speed until fluffy, 1-2 minutes. Reduce speed to low. Add 4 cups of sugar, milk, and vanilla. Mix on low until smooth. If the frosting is thin, add more sugar.

Frosting can be refrigerated for up to 3 days. Bring to room temperature before spreading on cake.

Variation

½ cup unsalted butter or shortening, softened

3 ounces cream cheese, softened (for dairy-free, substitute with shortening)

½ cup smooth peanut butter, softened

2-3 cups confectioners' sugar

¼ teaspoon vanilla extract

2-4 tablespoons milk or milk substitute

PEANUT BUTTER CREAM CHEESE FROSTING

Follow directions for *Best Cream Cheese Frosting* above, adding the peanut butter with the butter and cream cheese.

Chocolate Ganache

½ cup (4 ounces) semisweet chocolate chips or semisweet chocolate bar

¼ cup heavy cream or milk substitute like coconut milk

This recipe is excellent on the Chocolate Brownies (see Index) but it's equally as good on cake or cupcakes. Double it if you need more.

Makes enough to frost one 8" × 8" pan of brownies or about 12-15 cupcakes

Place the chocolate chips and cream into a microwave safe bowl. Microwave on high in 30 second intervals until melted, stirring in between. Alternatively, place chocolate and cream in a small saucepan. Heat on low until melted, stirring every few minutes. Use immediately. Spread over cake or brownies. To make them a little fancy, drag a fork across the frosting to make a lined pattern.

Chef Tips: Cookies

Rotate baking pans halfway during the baking process, switching from the top to the bottom position and vice versa. This will help the cookies bake more evenly.

Bake most cookies until they are golden brown on the edges. This makes them a little crisper, too.

Cool for at least 3 minutes before removing to minimize the cookies from breaking. Some cookies need to cool fully before removing.

If you have to roll out cookies, use potato starch; the cookies will be much less gritty.

To prevent the cookies from sticking to the pan, always line a baking sheet with a silicone baking mat or parchment paper.

Chocolate Chip Cookies

1¼ cups *Amy's Gluten-Free Flour Blend*
1 cup brown rice flour
2 tablespoons cornstarch
½ rounded teaspoon xanthan gum
1 teaspoon kosher salt
1 teaspoon baking soda

1 cup unsalted butter or shortening, melted and cooled slightly
½ cup white sugar
¾ cup light brown sugar
1 large egg
1 large egg yolk
2 tablespoons whole milk or milk substitute
1½ teaspoons vanilla extract
12 ounces (1 bag) semi-sweet chocolate chips

This recipe is adapted from one from Alton Brown of the Food Network. I used more of my own mix and adjusted the amount and type of sugar. Melting the butter is a great technique and produces a cookie which is crisp on the outside and chewy on the inside. If you are not going to eat these within 3 days, put them in the freezer in an air tight bag or container. Remove from freezer and within about 5-10 minutes, the cookie will be ready (or microwave for 10-15 seconds).

Makes 2–3 dozen

1. Mix the dry ingredients (first 6 ingredients) in a medium bowl. Set aside.
2. In the bowl of a stand mixer fitted with the paddle attachment, add the cooled butter and the white and brown sugar. You can also use a hand-held electric mixer with beaters. Beat the butter and sugars on medium speed for 1 minute until creamy.
3. Add the whole egg, egg yolk, milk and vanilla extract and mix until well combined.
4. Add half of the flour mixture and blend on low speed until combined. Add the other half of the flour and mix until fully blended. Give the mixture one quick twirl on medium for 10 seconds to help set the batter.
5. Add the chocolate chips. Mix on low until combined.
6. Chill the dough in the refrigerator until firm, approximately 1 hour.
7. Preheat the oven to 375°F. Prepare 2-3 baking sheets by lining with parchment paper or silicone baking mats.
8. Scoop out rounded tablespoons and place on the sheets, arranging about 9-12 cookies per sheet.
9. Bake for 16-18 minutes, rotating the pans after 8 minutes. Make sure cookies are browned and slightly firm on the edges.
10. Remove from the oven and cool the cookies on the pans for at least 3 minutes. Carefully, move the cookies to a wire rack and cool completely. Store cooked cookies in an airtight container or in the freezer in a freezer-safe bag.

Rolled Sugar Cookies

1   cup white rice flour
½   cup tapioca flour
1   cup cornstarch
1   teaspoon baking powder
2½   teaspoons xanthan gum
1   teaspoon kosher salt

1   cup white sugar
½   cup vegetable shortening
½   cup unsalted butter (use all shortening for dairy-free)
1   large egg
2   teaspoons vanilla extract
¼   cup potato starch, for kneading

Sprinkles for decorating

Chef Tip

Although there isn't any gluten in the batter, the dough can still be tough if too much potato starch is used.

Whether or not you are a kid, a rolled sugar cookie in some fun shape with colored sprinkles always seems fun. Don't be discouraged when you see pre-made cookies in the store; this recipe is easy and delicious (and might even taste better!). The original recipe came from www.food.com but I've made some adjustments to it. This is one exception where you need to use the flours listed instead of the mix; it makes it much lighter.

Makes 3-4 dozen, depending upon the size of the cookie cutter

1. Preheat oven to 350°F. Prepare 2-3 baking sheets by lining with parchment paper or silicone baking mats.
2. In a small bowl, mix together dry ingredients (first 6 ingredients).
3. In the bowl of a stand mixer fitted with the paddle attachment, cream together sugar, butter and shortening. Add the egg and vanilla and mix briefly. Add the dry ingredients, and mix to combine.
4. Take the bowl out of the mixer. Add ¼ cup of the potato starch and mix with your hands until it is well combined and not too sticky. Add more if necessary and use the rest for rolling. If the dough seems very sticky, place in the fridge for 10 minutes.
5. Divide the dough in half. Place some potato starch on the counter and put dough on top. Place more potato starch on top and roll out to about ⅛ inch thickness. Use more starch so the dough does not stick to the rolling pin or counter. Make sure the dough thickness is consistent so the cookies bake evenly.
6. Using cookie cutters, cut into shapes and place on pan. Optionally decorate with sprinkles before baking.
7. Re-use the scraps and roll out again, but try not to handle too much.
8. Bake for about 8-10 minutes, rotating once. Cool for at least 3 minutes before removing from the pan. Cool on wire racks.

Raspberry Linzer Cookies

1   recipe gluten-free rolled
    sugar cookies
½   cup raspberry preserves, like
    Grandma Hoener's™ or jelly,
    at room temperature
¼   cup confectioners' sugar

Makes about 2 dozen

1. Roll cookies out according to directions in recipe.
2. You will need two heart shaped cookies for each linzer cookie. Cut the first larger heart shaped cookie and place on one baking sheet. Cut the second heart shaped cookie in the same size. Then, using a smaller heart shaped cookie cutter, cut the inside of the cookie out. You can bake the smaller heart shape for mini cookies. Place the cut out cookie on another baking sheet (these bake quicker because of the cut-out).
3. Follow directions in recipe for baking and cooling cookies.
4. Once cool, place the cookies on a plate. Using a teaspoon or pastry brush, spread a thin layer of the raspberry preserves over the heart shaped cookie. Top with the cookie with the heart shaped cut-out. Dust with confectioners' sugar using a sifter or small mesh strainer.
5. Store covered at room temperature for up to 3 days or store in the freezer.

Shortbread

2 cups *Amy's Gluten-Free Flour Blend*
½ cup white rice flour plus extra for rolling
1 teaspoon xanthan gum
½ teaspoon kosher salt

1 cup unsalted butter, softened, or vegetable shortening
½ cup white sugar
1 teaspoon vanilla extract

You will be amazed at how much these taste like regular shortbread. The key is to not overwork the dough. We made these in a cooking class and the xanthan gum was omitted. Yes, the cookies fell apart but were still delicious! I'm sure this would be a good base for a tart but try it first. Make a cuppa tea and enjoy (no, not a typo; an English term).

Makes about 24-30 cookies

1. Preheat the oven to 325°F. Prepare 2 baking sheets with parchment paper or silicone baking mats.
2. In a bowl, mix the flours, xanthan gum, and salt together with a whisk. Set aside.
3. In a stand up mixer or with beaters, beat the softened butter and sugar until it just comes together, being careful not to overmix. Add vanilla and mix briefly.
4. Add the flour and mix until it is combined well. It might look crumbly at first, but keep mixing and it will come together.
5. Place dough on the counter. Use some white rice flour to keep from sticking. Roll into a log. Using a knife or pastry cutter, cut circles approximately ½" thick. You may need to pat them to make them more round. Place on baking sheets.
6. Bake for 12-14 minutes, rotating pans once. Cookies should be just golden on the edges.
7. Remove from oven and let rest for 3-5 minutes. Carefully remove from baking sheets, using a spatula, and place on a rack to cool. They can crumble easily but are so good!

Variation

LEMON SHORTBREAD

Add 2 tablespoons of lemon zest to the dough in step 4.

Lemon Almond Cookies

¾ cup *Amy's Gluten-Free Flour Blend*
½ cup **almond meal**
½ cup **cornstarch**
¼ teaspoon **kosher salt**
½ teaspoon **xanthan gum**

¾ cup **unsalted butter or shortening, softened**
1 cup plus 2 tablespoons **white sugar**
1 large **egg**
1½ tablespoons **freshly grated lemon zest (about 1 lemon)**

Many years ago, I had found a recipe for Lemon Almond Cookies, which had come from Gourmet Magazine, February 1990. I kept the hand written recipe card, with my own interpretation and instructions. At Christmas, I always made these delicious, sweet and crisp cookies. I'm not sure of the last time I made them but in recent years, with a gluten-free diet, I hadn't even attempted them. I just couldn't take it and decided to convert the recipe myself. My palate is fairly fine-tuned so I'm pretty good at distinguishing flavors. These hit the mark 100%. They are perfect with tea or for a Holiday party.

Makes 3 dozen cookies

1. In a small bowl, mix dry ingredients (first 5 ingredients).
2. In the bowl of a stand mixer, cream together the butter and 1 cup of the sugar for 2 minutes until fluffy. Scrape down the sides.
3. Beat in the egg and the zest until well blended, scraping down the sides.
4. Add the flour and mix on low until the dough is combined well. Raise the speed to medium and mix for 20 seconds.
5. Cover and chill for 1-2 hours in the fridge.
6. Preheat oven to 350°F. Prepare 2 baking sheets by lining with parchment paper or silicone baking mats.
7. Form the dough into walnut-size balls and arrange them 2 inches apart on baking sheets.
8. Place the remaining 2 tablespoons of sugar on a plate. Dip the bottom of a moistened glass in the sugar and press down on the cookies, flattening them to about 2 inches in diameter.
9. Bake the cookies for 12-15 minutes, or until they are golden around the edges, rotating pans halfway through the baking time.
10. Allow to cool for 5 minutes then transfer them to wire racks.

Ginger Molasses Cookies

1½ cups **Amy's Gluten-Free Flour Blend**
½ cup white rice flour
½ teaspoon xanthan gum
¾ teaspoon baking soda
½ teaspoon kosher salt
2 teaspoons ground ginger
1 teaspoon cinnamon
1 teaspoon ground cloves

¼ cup unsalted butter, softened (for dairy-free, use all shortening)
¼ cup vegetable shortening
½ cup brown sugar
¼ cup agave nectar or ⅓ cup brown or white sugar
1 large egg
¼ cup molasses
1 teaspoon apple cider vinegar
½ cup crystallized ginger, chopped

⅓ cup white sugar for rolling

My friend Corrine is well known for her ginger molasses cookies. I remember one meeting I was at with her when she brought them, and I had to pass. I decided to take her recipe and make a gluten-free version. It's nothing short of delicious, especially if you like the ginger flavor. Be careful though; they can be addictive!

Makes about 2 dozen

1. In a small bowl, mix dry ingredients (first 8 ingredients).
2. In a stand mixer, beat the softened butter, shortening and sugar until it just comes together, being careful not to overmix.
3. Add the egg, molasses, and apple cider vinegar. Mix to combine, scraping down the sides.
4. Slowly, stir in the dry ingredients until the mixture is just blended, then add the crystallized ginger.
5. Remove paddle and place bowl with cookie batter in the fridge for 30 minutes.
6. Preheat oven to 325°F. Prepare 2 baking sheets by lining with parchment paper or silicone baking mats.
7. Roll the dough into small balls (about one inch). Roll in sugar and then place on a cookie sheet lined with a silicone mat or parchment paper about 2 inches apart.
8. Bake the cookies for 15 minutes until puffed and golden, and slightly brown on the edges. Cool 5 minutes before removing.

Chocolate Crackle Cookies

¼ cup unsalted butter or vegetable shortening
3 squares (3 ounces) unsweetened chocolate

1 cup *Amy's Gluten-Free Flour Blend*
1 teaspoon baking powder
¼ teaspoon kosher salt
¼ teaspoon xanthan gum

1 cup + 3 tablespoons white sugar
2 large eggs
1 teaspoon vanilla

OPTIONAL INGREDIENTS:
25-30 Hershey's Kisses®, unwrapped

This cookie recipe is another blast from the past. How I missed them…until I tried them with my gluten-free flour blend and xanthan gum. Success!

Makes 2½ to 3 dozen cookies

1. Melt butter or shortening and chocolate (in the microwave, in 30 second intervals, or in a glass or metal bowl over a pot of simmering water). Transfer to a medium to large bowl and cool.
2. In a medium bowl, combine flour blend, baking powder, salt and xanthan gum.
3. In the bowl with the chocolate mixture, add 1 cup of sugar, eggs, and vanilla and mix well. Stir in flour mix until blended. Cover and chill in the fridge 60-90 minutes or until dough is firm enough to shape.
4. Preheat oven to 300°F. Prepare 2-3 baking sheets by lining with parchment paper or silicone baking mats.
5. Portion pieces of the dough which are slightly larger than a tablespoon. Roll into a ball and then roll in the remaining sugar. The dough gets sticky.
6. Place 2 inches apart on baking sheets. Bake 18-20 minutes or until crackled on top and firm to touch. Baking them longer will make the cookies more crunchy; less time will keep them soft in the middle.
7. Place cookie sheet on wire rack and cool the cookies on the sheet for at least 10 minutes before removing. Using a spatula, transfer cookies to the rack. Cool cookies completely.

VARIATION
If using Hershey's Kisses®, place cookie sheet on wire rack. Immediately place kiss on each cookie pressing down slightly. Wait until kisses are firm until removing cookie from the baking sheet.

Cinnamon Almond Biscotti

¾ cup *Amy's Gluten-Free Flour Blend*
½ cup almond flour
¼ cup sorghum flour
2 teaspoons baking powder
1 teaspoon xanthan gum
¼ teaspoon kosher salt
1 teaspoon cinnamon

8 tablespoons unsalted butter or vegetable shortening, softened
½ cup brown sugar
¼ cup white sugar
2 large eggs
½ cup sliced almonds, not toasted

This is often how things work with me. I decide at some point that I want something. Pizza, cookies, a madeleine… and since I'm eating a gluten-free diet, I can't always go to the store to buy it. Or, maybe I can but it's not always good. So it was, that day when I really wanted a good biscotti. Believe it or not, I've never even made them, even with gluten! The next part of the journey began with finding the right recipe. I wasn't in the mood for lemon pecan or orange walnut. I didn't want chocolate either. Cinnamon almond was coming to mind so that's what I decided to try to create. I adapted a recipe from the blog GlutenFreeGirl with my own ingredients and slightly different method. I have served these to many people and the results are always the same. They cannot believe they are gluten-free.

Makes 3 to 4 dozen cookies

1. Preheat oven to 350°F. Prepare 2 baking sheets by lining with parchment paper or silicone baking mats.
2. Place the dry ingredients (first 7 ingredients) in a medium bowl. Using a whisk, mix until well blended. If necessary, use your fingers to break up any big pieces of almond flour or baking powder. Set aside.
3. Put the butter in a stand mixer. Using the paddle attachment, beat the butter for about a minute and then pour in the sugar. Cream the butter and sugar together until the batter is smooth, about 3 minutes. Add the eggs one at a time until the mixture is fluffy.
4. With the mixture on low, add the dry ingredients in 3 batches. Turn the speed to medium and mix for 30 seconds. This helps to "gel" the xanthan gum and hold the dough together. Lower the speed and add the almonds until just mixed. The dough will be sticky.
5. You can either use an ice cream scoop or greased spatula to place the dough on one of the baking sheets in two long rows (save the second baking sheet for later). Pat down and form each into its own long log with a spatula. It should be a little flat as well. And yes, it will be sticky.
6. Bake the biscotti for 16-18 minutes, turning around once. Bake until golden and somewhat firm, but still somewhat soft, pushing the top center of the cookie.
7. Remove from oven. Cool biscotti on the tray for 10 minutes. Carefully move each log to a wire rack and leave for at least 30 minutes to firm up.
8. Heat oven to 350°F again. When the biscotti are entirely cool, place one log on a cutting board. With a serrated knife, cut consistent slices, about ½" wide, depending upon how you like your cookies. Move them back onto the same baking sheet from step 6, bottom side down and repeat with the other log, using the second baking sheet.
9. Once the oven is hot, place biscotti back into oven. Bake until they are lightly toasted and crunchy, about 18 minutes (for thinner sliced biscotti) to 22 minutes (for wider sliced biscotti), rotating the pans once. Be careful not to overcook them or else they will have a burnt taste.
10. Cool entirely. Store in an airtight container.

Variations

CRANBERRY WALNUT

Omit cinnamon from dry ingredients and add 1 extra tablespoon of gluten-free flour mix. Add 1 teaspoon vanilla extract with the eggs. Omit almonds. Add ½ cup dried cranberries to the flour mix. Add ½ cup chopped walnuts to the dough in place of the almonds in step 4.

MOCHA CHOCOLATE CHIP

Omit cinnamon from dry ingredients and add 1 extra tablespoon of gluten-free flour mix. Add 1 teaspoon vanilla extract with the eggs. Omit almonds.
Add 2 tablespoons instant coffee to the dry ingredients in step 2.
Add 1 cup chocolate chips to the dough in place of the almonds in step 4.

Chocolate Brownies

½   **cup semi-sweet chocolate chips**
2   **ounces bittersweet chocolate**
¼   **cup unsalted butter or vegetable oil**

2   **large eggs (use 3 for more**
     of a cake-like brownie)
¾   **cup white sugar (you can use less**
     sugar if you prefer it less sweet)
1   **teaspoon vanilla**

½   **cup *Amy's Gluten-Free Flour Blend***
½   **teaspoon kosher salt**
½   **cup semi-sweet chocolate chips**

Makes 8" × 8" square pan

1. In a microwave safe bowl, place chocolate chips, bittersweet chocolate and butter or oil. In 30 second intervals, microwave butter and chocolates, stirring in between until chocolate is melted. Alternatively, place both chocolates and butter or oil in a bowl and place over a pot of simmering water to melt chocolate. Allow to cool for 10-15 minutes.

2. Preheat oven to 325°F. Most brownie recipes call for a temperature of 350°F. This lower temperature helps to cook the brownies more evenly and prevent the edges from getting dried out. Grease pan. You can also line the pan with foil if you want to be able to remove the whole brownie from the pan, and then cut into pieces. Grease the foil if you use that option.

3. In another bowl, whisk eggs, sugar and vanilla until smooth. Add the cooled chocolate from step 1 and mix with the whisk.

4. Add flour, salt and chocolate chips and mix with a spatula until blended (the chocolate chips tend to get stuck in the whisk). Pour into the pan and use a spatula to get out every last drop.

5. Bake about 25-28 minutes. It's done when you can smell the chocolate and a toothpick inserted in the middle has moist chocolate on it but is neither dry nor very wet. Brownies should pull away from the sides slightly.

6. Cool for at least 15 minutes.

7. Optionally frost with *Chocolate Ganache* (see Index).

MOCHA ALMOND

Add 2 tablespoons instant espresso or coffee powder to step 4. Frost brownies with *Chocolate Ganache* and top with ¾ cup sliced almonds, toasted.

Variation

Cooking Lesson

HOW TO MAKE PIE CRUST
(full recipe follows on next page)

1. Place dry ingredients in food processor and mix.

2. Place cold butter and/or shortening in the processor.

3. Process until butter is incorporated and the mixture looks like grated cheese. Alternatively, "cut" the butter with the flour in a bowl with two knives or a pastry blender.

4. Transfer to mixing bowl and add liquid ingredients. Start by adding 1 table-spoon of water.

5. Mix dough with your hands. Add more water until it comes together.

6. Shape into a disc.

7. Crust should be smooth or else it will crack. Wrap in plastic and place in the fridge for at least 30 minutes.

8. Roll between plastic wrap. You can also use a special silicone rolling mat which the dough will not stick to.

9. You can also use *Amy's Gluten-Free Flour Blend* to roll out the dough.

10. Carefully roll the dough onto the roll-ing pin to transfer it to the pie dish.

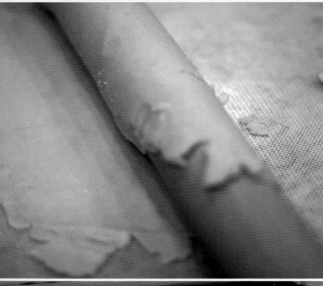

Chef Tips: Pie Crust

- Cut the butter into ½" cubes to make it easier to distribute before processing. You don't need to do this with the shortening since it's softer.
- When mixing the pie crust, if it is very sticky, add more of the flour blend so that it is tacky. If it is breaking, add a few drops of cold water. Developing the right texture of pie crust takes practice.
- Shape the dough based on the recipe (either 1 or 2 discs) and wrap in plastic. Place in fridge for at least 30 minutes or up to 4 days. This helps the butter or shortening to firm back up.
- Remove the crust from the fridge about 5 minutes before you are ready to use it. If you only need one piece, reserve the other piece for later use.
- To roll, place the disc between two sheets of plastic. If the dough seems sticky, use a little potato starch or *Amy's Gluten-Free Flour Blend* on the dough so it doesn't stick to the plastic.
- You can also roll on the counter. Place about 2 teaspoons of the starch or flour blend on the counter. Place dough on top. Place a piece of plastic on top of the dough and roll. Flip dough over once to make sure both sides are not too sticky. Use more starch if necessary.
- If it's hard to roll out, leave it on the counter for another 5 minutes. If the dough is still hard to roll, it does not have enough water. You can try patting the dough with water to fix it.
- Roll out to ⅛" thick. If using 2 sheets of plastic, remove top piece of plastic. Flip dough into the baking dish or pan and remove other piece of plastic.
- If you rolled on the counter, use the rolling pin to roll the dough back onto the pin. This makes it easier to unroll into the pie dish or pan. Use more starch if the dough is sticky.
- If the dough breaks, press together to mend.

USES FOR EXTRA DOUGH

Pastry leaves: With some of the extra dough, roll out. Using mini leaf cookie cutters (or a paring knife), cut, and place on a baking sheet lined with parchment paper or a silicone baking mat. Use a small knife to make lines on the leaf. Brush with an egg wash (use the same one from any of the pie recipes). Bake at 400°F until golden, maybe 7-10 minutes. Once cool, place on top of pie, for example, a pumpkin pie.

Pastry twists: Roll out dough. Cut into strips 5-6" long. Twist and place on a baking sheet lined with parchment paper or a silicone baking mat. Sprinkle with white sugar and cinnamon. Bake at 400°F until golden, maybe 7-10 minutes or until golden and fragrant.

Pie Crust

4   **tablespoons unsalted butter,
cut into ½" cubes**
4   **tablespoons vegetable shortening**
**Note: You can use all butter, or,
for dairy-free, all shortening**

1¾   **cups *Amy's Gluten-Free Flour
Blend* plus extra if necessary**
¾   **teaspoon xanthan gum**
½   **teaspoon sea or kosher salt**

1   **large egg, lightly beaten**
2   **teaspoons white or apple
cider vinegar**
1-2 **tablespoons ice water**

**Potato starch or *Amy's Gluten-
Free Flour Blend* for rolling**

*Makes 2 crusts (top and a bottom) for pie, quiche or any crust you
might need*

1. Before you begin, see *Chef Tips: Pie Crust* on opposite page. Place
butter and shortening in a small bowl in the freezer to get extra
cold. It only needs to be in there for 5 minutes. By the time you are
done measuring the flours, it will be cold enough.
2. Add flour, xanthan gum, and salt to a food processor. Pulse a few
times to mix. Alternatively, mix this in a medium bowl.
3. Add very cold shortening and butter to the processor. Pulse for
10-20 seconds or until shortening and butter are chopped. The
mixture should look like grated Parmesan cheese. If you don't have
a food processor, use a pastry blender to blend the butter and
shortening with the flour mixture, or use two knifes to "cut" the
shortening and butter into the flour mixture.
4. Mix the egg and vinegar in a medium bowl. Add the butter and
flour mixture and 1 tablespoon of the ice water. Reserve the last
tablespoon if needed.
5. Using your hands, mix the dough. Wait to add more water until
the dough has begun to take shape. Shape according to the recipe
(either 1 or 2 discs). Dough should stick together well and should
not have cracks. If it does have cracks or is dry, add a few drops of
water until it doesn't have cracks and isn't dry.

Sweet Pie Crust

4   **tablespoons unsalted butter,
cut into ½" cubes**
4   **tablespoons vegetable shortening**
**Note: You can use all butter, or,
for dairy-free, all shortening**

1¾   **cups *Amy's Gluten-Free Flour
Blend* plus extra if necessary**
3   **tablespoons white sugar**
2   **tablespoons corn or potato starch**
1   **teaspoon xanthan gum**
½   **teaspoon kosher salt**

1   **egg, lightly beaten**
2   **teaspoons white or apple cider vinegar**
1-2 **tablespoons ice water**

**Potato starch or *Amy's Gluten-
Free Flour Blend* for rolling**

*Makes 2 crusts (top and bottom) for apple pie, fruit galette or any other
sweet pie*

Follow the directions for *Pie Crust* above. Add sugar and corn or
potato starch to the flour blend in step 2.

Pumpkin Pie

1   recipe Pie Crust (see Index)

FILLING

1   15-ounce can pumpkin puree (not pumpkin pie filling)
½   cup heavy cream or milk substitute
¼-½ cup brown sugar or cane sugar
¼   cup agave nectar (or use all sugar)
2   eggs (if you don't use heavy cream, use 3 eggs)
1   teaspoon cinnamon
½   teaspoon kosher salt
½   teaspoon ground ginger
½   teaspoon nutmeg
¼   teaspoon cloves

Egg wash: 1 egg mixed with 1 teaspoon milk or water, lightly beaten

Chef Tips

I normally make this recipe in a deep dish pie crust which can fit 4 cups of liquid without the crust; regular pie dishes can only hold 3-3½ cups. You can choose to make it in the deeper pie dish or to make it in two regular pie dishes.

If you make it in a single 9" dish, you will have extra filling. You can always place the filling in a small greased ramekin to make a pumpkin pudding. Bake it for 20 minutes or until set in the middle.

If you use two 9" pans, it won't be filled to the top but you will have two pies.

When I used to bake with gluten, this was one of my signature dishes. I was able to play with the gluten free ingredients and method to come up with something pretty close. This version is made with heavy cream but that can be substituted with a milk substitute; just add an extra egg. You can also reduce the sugar if necessary. Either way, it's a wonderful recipe that can be made year round; don't wait until the fall!

Makes one 9" deep dish pie or two 9" regular pies

1. Prepare crust. Shape into 1 or 2 discs, depending upon how many pies you are making (see *Chef Tips* to the left).
2. Remove pie crust 5 minutes prior to using. Roll out to 1/8" (refer to pie crust instructions) and place dough into pie dish. Cut excess with kitchen scissors or a knife. Reserve extra to make pretty leaves or pastry twists (see *Chef Tips* on prior page).
3. Crimp edges and place back in the fridge for 20 minutes to harden the dough. This prevents the dough from shrinking too much when baked in the hot oven.
4. Mix filling ingredients in a large bowl.
5. Preheat oven to 425°F. Remove crust from fridge. Pour filling into shell. Brush egg wash on the crust so it browns nicely. Sprinkle white sugar on top of this to make the crust a little sweeter and help with the browning.
6. Bake 15 minutes, then reduce oven temperature to 350°F and continue baking 35-40 minutes until knife inserted in center comes out clean. If the crust browns too quickly, place foil around the edges of the crust.
7. Cool before eating. Crust might be crumbly so cut with care.

VARIATION

Instead of heavy cream, agave nectar and brown sugar, use 1 can of condensed milk. Pumpkin pie will be lighter in color.

Apple Pie

1   recipe Pie Crust (see Index)

FILLING
4-5 tart apples, cored, peeled
     and sliced thinly
1   tablespoons cornstarch
     or tapioca starch
2-3 tablespoons white sugar (use
     more if the apples are tart)
1   teaspoon cinnamon
1   tablespoon lemon juice
2   teaspoon lemon zest (zest of about
     ½ lemon)

**Egg wash: 1 egg mixed with 1 teaspoon
milk or water, lightly beaten
1 teaspoon white sugar**

1. Prepare crust.
2. When crust is ready to be rolled, remove from fridge. Mix filling ingredients in a medium bowl.
3. Roll out both discs. Place one in the pie dish (see *Chef Tips* on prior page to learn about how to roll out the crust).
4. Place filling ingredients in pie dish. Dab water along the edge of the pie crust. Carefully place the second pie crust on top. Crimp edges together. Cut slits in top crust.
5. Mix egg wash and brush over top. Sprinkle with sugar.
6. Bake at 425°F for 10 minutes. Reduce heat to 350°F; bake 30-35 minutes more or until crust is golden and filling is bubbly. If the crust is getting dark, cover with foil to prevent burning.
7. Cool for 15 minutes before cutting.

Fruit Galette

⅔ recipe Sweet Pie Crust or Pie Crust (see Index)

3-4 apples (like Granny Smith) or pears, peeled, cored, cut into ⅛-inch-thick slices

2 teaspoons potato starch or *Amy's Gluten-Free Flour Blend*

3-4 tablespoons white sugar, divided
Pinch of salt

¼ cup apricot preserves (heat the preserves slightly to make it easier to spread)

Egg wash: 1 egg mixed with 1 teaspoon milk or water, lightly beaten

OPTIONAL INGREDIENTS:
½ teaspoon cinnamon
1 teaspoon finely grated lemon zest

NOTE:
Galette can be made with other fruit like peaches, nectarines or berries.

Chef Tip

Apples and pears brown when exposed to air. When making the galette, slice the fruit right before the crust is rolled out.

A galette is a rustic style pie with the middle left open. If you don't have the time or patience to make a pie or just want something different, try this. One tester said "What I especially liked was the ease of putting it together. Sometimes I won't bake a pie because I just don't have the time or patience for the crust. I love a pie to be beautiful and I take extra time for crimping or decorating the crust. The galette was fast and I loved the rustic French look."

Serves 6-8

1. Follow instructions for either pie crust but use 2/3 of the dough for the galette; this way you will have enough. See *Chef Tips: Pie Crust* on page 244 for ideas on what to do with remaining dough.

2. Preheat oven to 375°F.

3. Remove crust from fridge after apples or pears are peeled but before they are cut. In a medium bowl, combine apple or pear slices, cornstarch and cinnamon if using. Do not add the sugar or salt yet.

4. On the counter, roll the dough out to 1/8" thick round and about 13"-14" in diameter, making sure to use plenty of potato starch or flour blend to prevent sticking. It is very important that you can move the dough around without it sticking to the counter while you are rolling it; otherwise the galette might break and juices will run out and burn during baking. Alternatively, roll between 2 pieces of plastic wrap.

5. Using the rolling pin, roll the dough up onto itself and transfer it to the baking sheet, unrolling it onto the sheet. If you have used plastic wrap, peel 1 piece off and then flip the dough over onto prepared baking sheet. Remove the other piece of plastic.

6. With a spoon or pastry brush, spread the preserves in the center of the crust, making an approximate 10" circle.

7. To the fruit, add 2-3 tablespoons sugar depending upon sweetness of fruit, a pinch of salt and optionally lemon zest. Gently toss to blend.

8. Arrange fruit slices in circles atop preserves, overlapping slightly. If there is liquid in the bottom of the bowl, do not add to fruit.

9. Using the parchment to guide the dough, carefully fold crust border up over slices, leaving the center open. If the dough breaks, pinch together to mend. Brush crust with egg wash. Sprinkle crust with remaining tablespoon of sugar.

10. Bake galette 30-35 minutes until crust is golden brown. Remove from oven and cool at least 10 minutes.

11. To remove, slide long thin knife between parchment and galette and carefully transfer to serving dish. Cut into wedges and serve warm or at room temperature.

Fruit Crisp

CRISP TOPPING:

½ cup *Amy's Gluten-Free Flour Blend*

⅓ cup gluten-free oats (if you can't tolerate oats, substitute with the same amount of gluten-free flour)

⅓-½ cup white sugar or natural sweetener

½ teaspoon kosher salt

1 teaspoon ground cinnamon

½ cup chopped walnuts or pecans (optional)

6-8 tablespoons melted unsalted butter or vegetable oil (use more if you want a crisper topping)

FILLING:

4 cups sliced, peeled and cored fruit like apples, pears, peaches, nectarines and/or blueberries, blackberries or olallieberries (use all of one or a combination)

⅓-½ cup sugar or agave nectar (use more if the fruit is tart or if you use more than 4 cups of fruit)

2 tablespoons cornstarch

What I love about this recipe is that you can make it all year round. In the summer, there is a bounty of fruit like peaches, apricots, nectarines, and all types of berries. In the winter, you can use apples, pears, and frozen fruit. The recipe is very forgiving as well. You can measure the fruit or just put enough to fill your pan. Use what's on hand and check the freezer.

If you are concerned about the oats (some people can't even tolerate the gluten-free variety), add more gluten-free flour mix and chopped nuts. To save time, measure the crisp ingredients (except the butter) beforehand and keep it in a bowl until you are ready to bake. Instead of a store-bought dessert, why not give this one a try? I'll bet everyone will appreciate it!

Serves 6-8

1. Preheat the oven to 375°F. Grease a 2-2½-quart baking dish or deep pie dish.
2. Mix the Crisp Topping ingredients in a medium bowl until well blended. Set aside.
3. Mix the fruit, sugar and cornstarch and toss gently. Transfer the fruit mixture to the baking dish and cover with the crisp topping, spreading evenly.
4. Place in the oven and bake until the top is well browned and the fruit is tender when pierced with a knife, about 35-40 minutes.
5. Serve with whipped cream or ice cream. See Index for *Whipped Cream* recipe.

Variation

PEAR GINGER

Use 4 pears, peeled, cored and sliced for the fruit filling. Add ½ teaspoon ground ginger, ¼ teaspoon ground nutmeg and ½ cup slivered almonds (instead of walnuts or pecans) to the crisp topping. Follow directions above.

Lemon Tart

Crust:
½   **cup cold unsalted butter or vegetable shortening, cut into bits**
1   **cup *Amy's Gluten-Free Flour Blend***
½   **cup cornstarch**
¼   **cup confectioner's sugar**
1   **teaspoon xanthan gum**
Pinch of salt
1   **large egg, beaten**

Filling:
1   **cup white sugar**
3   **large eggs, lightly beaten**
2   **tablespoons cornstarch**
½   **teaspoon baking powder**
Juice of 1 lemon (about 2½ - 3 tablespoons)
Grated zest of 1 lemon

Confectioner's sugar for decoration

This is a favorite recipe that is light and tangy. Everyone seems to like it, regardless of their age (assuming they like lemon!). The egg in the crust helps it to hold together better. If you like your tart more tart, reduce the sugar in the filling to ¾ of a cup. The butter might leak a bit so I would suggest placing foil on the bottom of the tart pan and cooking on a baking sheet. One of my testers suggested using limes instead. I never got around to making it but it seems like it would work nicely.

Makes one 9" tart

1. Preheat oven to 350°F. Place a piece of foil on a baking sheet and then place a 9" tart pan with a removable bottom on top. This helps prevent the butter from leaking into the oven in case it comes out of the pan. You can also make this in an 8" × 8" square pan.
2. Place flour, cornstarch, xanthan gum, sugar, and salt in a food processor bowl and process until combined. Add the cold butter and process until it resembles grated cheese or coarse meal. If you don't have a food processor, mix the dry ingredients in a bowl and then cut in the butter with two knives or a pastry cutter.
3. Transfer the flour mixture from the processor to a medium bowl. Add the beaten egg and mix with a spatula. The dough will be crumbly and not in one piece.
4. Gently press the dough into the bottom and up the side of the pan.
5. Bake crust 16-18 minutes or until just becoming brown. Cool 10 minutes.
6. Do not blend the filling ingredients until the tart shell is cooled; the ingredients can be prepped. When the crust is slightly cooled, mix the filling ingredients with a whisk in a medium bowl and pour mixture into the partially baked tart shell. Bake the tart at 350°F for 20-25 minutes or until the crust is golden and the top is light brown.
7. Cool completely and remove sides of tart pan. If the crust is sticking, use a knife to gently loosen the tart from the sides.
8. The tart is better chilled but can be served at room temperature. Sprinkle confectioners' sugar on top before serving.

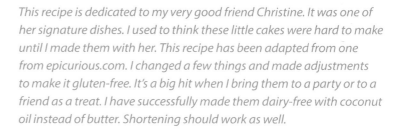

Vanilla Madeleines

1   **tablespoon softened, unsalted butter, or vegetable shortening for greasing the pan**

1   **tablespoon white rice flour (or *Amy's Gluten-Free Flour Blend*)**

2   **large eggs at room temperature, lightly beaten**

⅔   **cup white sugar**

2   **teaspoons vanilla extract**

1   **cup *Amy's Gluten-Free Flour Blend***

¼   **teaspoon xanthan gum**

¼   **teaspoon kosher salt or good pinch of regular salt**

10   **tablespoons unsalted butter, melted, cooled slightly (for dairy-free, use melted vegetable shortening or coconut oil)**

Confectioners' sugar (optional)

This recipe is dedicated to my very good friend Christine. It was one of her signature dishes. I used to think these little cakes were hard to make until I made them with her. This recipe has been adapted from one from epicurious.com. I changed a few things and made adjustments to make it gluten-free. It's a big hit when I bring them to a party or to a friend as a treat. I have successfully made them dairy-free with coconut oil instead of butter. Shortening should work as well.

Makes 20 medium madeleines

1. Preheat oven to 375°F. Generously butter and flour pan for large madeleines (about 3 × 1¼ inches).
2. Using electric mixer, beat eggs and ⅔ cup sugar in large bowl for 1 minute to blend. Beat on medium-high for about 30 seconds. Mix in vanilla.
3. Mix flour, xanthan gum and salt in a small bowl. Add to the batter; beat just until blended. Gradually add cooled melted butter in steady stream, beating just until blended. Beat on medium for 10 seconds or until mixed together. Scrape down the sides and mix one more time.
4. Portion 1 tablespoon of batter into each indentation in pan. Bake until puffed and brown, about 16-18 minutes. The cakes are done when they spring back when touched in the middle. Cool 5 minutes. Gently remove from pan.
5. Sift powdered sugar to decorate.

VARIATIONS

For Lemon Madeleines, add zest from one lemon with vanilla in step 2.

For *Chocolate Dipped Madeleines*, make Vanilla Madeleines above and cool. Melt 3 ounces of semi-sweet or bittersweet chocolate in a bowl over a pan of hot water or in the microwave, mixing every 30 seconds until melted. Dip each madeleine into the melted chocolate about halfway. Tap excess chocolate and place them on a baking sheet lined with wax paper or a parchment paper. Leave at room temperature. Chocolate should be set in about 1 hour.

Chocolate Molten Cakes

4 ounces semi-sweet chocolate chips
2 ounces unsweetened chocolate (you can use all bittersweet chocolate; if you do, use 1 tablespoon less sugar)
6 tablespoons unsalted butter or vegetable shortening

Butter or shortening and sugar to grease and coat ramekins (use cocoa powder or brown sugar in place of white sugar if you don't want to see white flecks when cake is inverted)

¼ cup white sugar
2 large eggs, lightly beaten
¼ cup *Amy's Gluten-Free Flour Blend*
1 teaspoon baking powder
¼-½ teaspoon kosher salt

This recipe can be doubled. Serves 4-6

1. Preheat oven to 375°F.
2. Melt chocolate and butter or shortening. To melt it in the microwave, place in a microwave-safe bowl and cook in 30 second intervals, stirring in between until smooth. You can also place chocolate and butter or shortening in a metal or glass bowl over a pot of simmering water, stirring occasionally. Once the chocolate is smooth and melted, set aside to cool.
3. Grease the sides and bottoms of 6-8 six ounce ramekins. Add a little sugar to each ramekin and tap ramekin until coated, removing excess sugar. Set aside.
4. In a medium bowl, mix the sugar and eggs. Add the cooled chocolate and and stir to combine. Add flour blend, baking powder, and salt. Whisk until smooth and thick. Divide mixture into ramekins.
5. Bake for 10-12 minutes or until middle is just barely set. If you use 8 ramekins (i.e. use less batter per ramekin), bake for 8-10 minutes. Remove from oven.
6. To invert, run a knife around the edge and place a serving plate on top. Flip ramekin over so cake is on plate. Serve with whipped cream or ice cream.
7. To make ahead, undercook by 2 minutes. Let them cool and reheat in the microwave for 45 seconds before serving.

Struffoli

1⅔ cups *Amy's Gluten-Free Flour Blend*
¾ teaspoon xanthan gum
Pinch of salt
3 tablespoons white sugar

6 egg yolks (save the whites for omelets, meringue or *Coconut Shrimp*-see Index)
¼ cup heavy cream or plain coconut creamer for dairy-free
1½ tablespoons Sambuca, rum, or vanilla

1-2 teaspoons each potato starch and white rice flour, mixed together, for dusting
Oil or shortening for frying (about ½-1 cup)

Honey or agave nectar
Non-pareils or colored sprinkles (make sure they are gluten-free)

Have you ever had a struffoli? To me, it says Christmas with my family. These little fried dough balls are coated with honey and sprinkled with non-pareils (those little colored balls). Struffoli are honey dough balls that many Italian families enjoy at Christmas. It seems the tradition is most popular in the southern part of Italy.
This dessert was part of my childhood. I missed them after going gluten-free but decided to try to convert the recipe. Once again, you would be hard-pressed to tell the difference. Even if you are not Italian, you and your family will surely enjoy this treat.

This recipe can be doubled. Makes about 3 cups

1. Mix the flour blend, xanthan gum, salt and the sugar in a large bowl. Make a well in the middle. Mix the egg yolks, ¼ cup of cream and Sambuca, rum, or vanilla in another small bowl.
2. Pour the egg mixture into the well of the flour mixture and stir until well combined. Use your hands to make a disc. If the dough does not stick together, add more cream, a few drops at a time. Dough should be tacky, bright yellow but not sticky. If it is sticky, use extra flour when rolling.
3. Cut the disc into 8 wedges. Keep covered while rolling. Place a little of the flour/starch mixture on the counter. Roll each wedge into a long log that is about ½" in diameter and about 16" long (a little smaller than a pretzel rod in diameter, maybe twice the length). If the dough seems like it is separating, squeeze together. With a knife, cut the log into small pieces about ½".
4. Place some flour/starch on a cookie sheet and place the dough on the sheet until ready to fry.
5. When all of the dough is rolled out, heat a large pot to medium-high and add oil. I have used a Dutch oven as well as a large sauce pan which I tilted to the side. The dough has to be immersed. When the oil is hot, place one dough ball in the oil to test. It should bubble a bit and roll around.
6. Working in batches, fry all of the dough balls. Place on a plate lined with paper towels or a brown paper bag to absorb the oil. Cool and keep covered. Refrigerate after 1 day.
7. When ready to serve, place in a large bowl and pour honey or agave nectar on top (I used both) and stir to coat. Top with sprinkles and serve in individual bowls.

Index

V

W

X

Y

Z